This book is dedicated to Stuart Gronow who inspired the work reported in these pages and who acted as mentor and 'guiding hand'.

Contents

Preface

This book is concerned with the valuation of residential properties for owner occupation in the United Kingdom. If appraisal is defined as including both the physical survey of property and its valuation, the primary focus here is on the latter. It is concerned only in passing with the surveying of properties that forms the other essential part of appraisal. Surveying is a distinct discipline and residential survey is well served by numerous texts (see for example, Melville and Gordon, 1992; Williams, 1993).

The book aims to present a critique of current valuation theory and practice, to offer suggestions for the development of the traditional valuation method and to present the outlines of supplementary approaches that can take advantage of advances in technology and the growth of available data.

The latter relies on an exploration of new technological and statistical techniques. These are described in non-technical language in the body of the book and are supplemented by a more 'technical' appendix for those who wish either to pursue the development of such techniques or provide a critique of the approaches developed here.

A second focus of the book is the market for appraisal advice. This part of the book is concerned with structural changes that have occurred in the appraisal profession in the UK and with the interests of both purveyors and consumers of professional advice. It is also concerned with the rapid development of new techniques and e-commerce. This component of the book is both descriptive and prescriptive, though the prescriptive elements are tentative and invite discussion.

Findings are based on empirical and theoretical work, both academic research and consultancy, conducted by researchers at the University of Glamorgan over several years.

It is tempting to suggest that research is a purely objective pursuit and that research findings are always impartial. This temptation has been avoided in deference to valuers, who are trained to give opinions and identify an opinion when they see one.

Consequently, as far as practicable, opinion is distinguished from empirical observation in the text.

Motivation for this book

Four distinct perspectives are offered that have motivated the research reported in this book.

Professional perspective

A key motive for research is professional self-interest and development. One of the questions in the minds of practitioners throughout the last decade has been, 'in what form will this profession survive?'

While residential appraisal as a professional discipline has received too little attention, the business of residential appraisal has been changing rapidly. Professional residential surveying businesses have been and are vulnerable to encroachment by competitors of various kinds. Financial institutions, estate agents, building surveyors, solicitors, accountants and more recently software houses have ranked among the predators.

Alongside competitive fears, a natural fear also exists that the distinctive role of surveyors may be eroded. For example, structural transformation within lending organisations has brought considerable changes to appraisal business (see Chapter 3) and both government review and technological advance promise even deeper change.

Taken together these factors produce a stressful climate for the conduct of business. Moreover, fears appear to have been justified given the decline in the number of independent professional firms and a recent upswing in investment in newer technologies following a prolonged period of avoidance.

Of course, another equally healthy motive for research is the desire to offer top-rate service to the consumer. Many professional firms have undertaken research programmes, supported academic research and contributed specifically to the research described in this book.

Consumer perspective

There are three problems confronting consumers of valuation advice.

• Appraisal practice may be poor. It is on behalf of lending institutions that surveyors have conducted most residential mortgage valuation business. It must be inferred from the development of this business over the last decade that the lending institutions have not been satisfied with the quality of advice received from independent firms. During this period, the lenders have established their own valuation teams and regulated the market for the provision of independent advice through an ever more stringent 'panel' system.

- Appraisal practice may not be independent. The lenders regulate this market for valuation in their own interests. During the last decade, the consumer – the purchaser of property – received valuation advice only vicariously in over 90% of cases. As a consequence institutional interests have taken priority over the interests of the consumer. As shall be illustrated, institutional and consumer interests are not identical.
- The valuation method may be deficient. The standard method for the deduction of value has stood unchanged for decades despite evidence of periodic failure and no systematic review of this method has been undertaken.

It is my opinion that the consumer needs to be the principal client of professional valuers and that the interests of consumers are best protected when directly receiving good quality, independent professional advice.

From this statement it should be clear that I also assume and believe that, objectively, consumers require a service and that this service can be provided. No doubt exists about this in the minds of our American colleagues: 'The future need for appraising is obvious...' (Miller and Gallagher, 1998).

Social perspective

UK housing markets of the late 1980s and 1990s experienced dramatic and unpredicted rises and falls in asset values. Consequent social and economic problems evidenced by negative equity, repossessions and personal bankruptcy fuelled renewed academic, professional and political interest in the relationship between housing markets and the economy generally. However, no concerted or structured approach to tackling the issue was adopted.

Certainly within the appraisal discipline different aspects of the problem were reviewed. But the motivation was not to address problems at the social level.

A review of appraisal practice was carried out by the Royal Institution of Chartered Surveyors (RICS, 1994). Consequently guidance to valuers was revised through the merger of the Red and White Books into the *RICS Appraisal and Valuation Manual* (RICS, 1995). Surveying firms and lending institutions also devoted some energy to a review of practice and the research team had direct experience of this phenomenon through consultancy.

These reviews were inspired by business needs and dared not raise key questions about the social role of valuers who had consistently approved valuations as markets soared then collapsed.

Given that fundamentally the valuation method has remained unchanged, there would appear a risk that valuations are as socially useful now as they were in 1989. Nevertheless, objectively, valuations ought to perform a socially useful role in regulating lending/borrowing as economic basics suggest – a further argument in favour of independent professional advice.

In my opinion, valuation methods and practice have not kept pace with changing social needs.

Academic perspective

Removed from the practical difficulties of providing over a million valuations every year to residential consumers in the UK, academics wonder why practitioners do things the way they do and fail to use a variety of other means that academics have had time to ponder but never use in anger.

Academics in real estate appraisal are concerned about theories of value (though the literature on this generated by real estate academics is sparse), definitions and measures of value or worth, valuation methods and practice, appraisal standards and ethics. In a memorable paper, one American real estate professor (Kelly, 1990) explained that the academic must be concerned with the purposive (what for) and the normative (so what). These are the concerns of this book.

David Jenkins
February 2000

References

Kelly, H. (1990) 'Can universities teach real estate decision making?', *Real Estate Review*, Summer, 78–84.

Melville, I.A. and Gordon, I.A. (1992) *Structural Surveys of Dwelling Houses: Including Capital Surveys of Flats and New Dwellings*. London: Estates Gazette.

Miller, H. and Gallagher, K.R. (1998) *Residential Real Estate Appraisal*, 3rd edn. Prentice Hall.

RICS (1994) *The Mallinson Report*. London: RICS.

RICS (1995) *RICS Appraisal and Valuation Manual*. London: RICS.

Williams, A.R. (1993) *Domestic Building Surveys*. London: E & FN Spon.

Acknowledgments

In writing this book I am conscious of the fact that it represents the output of a team effort that was inspired by Stuart Gronow, now Professor Emeritus in Real Estate Appraisal at the University of Glamorgan. I wish to record my thanks for the opportunity of reporting this research effort and acknowledge my indebtedness to all of my colleagues.

Initially Stuart encouraged research into the application of artificial intelligence techniques to residential appraisal. Dr Ian Scott, who analysed the decision-making processes of valuers and reproduced them in a pilot expert system (1998), conducted the early work. Dr Hadi Nawawi and I later took up the challenge under Stuart's guiding hand and produced respectively a methodology for integrating expertise in a domain occupied by a multiplicity of experts (1998) and a functional expert database system tailored to value social housing (1992).

The research effort subsequently benefited from a substantial injection of funds from the private sector and a grant from the Economic and Social Research Council.

Consequently Raymond Dennett obtained an MPhil, while Nigel Almond, Owen Lewis and Panayiotis Panayiotou were all awarded doctorates in 1999. Jaqueline Daly has recently transferred from MPhil to PhD and is due to complete during the next year. It has been my privilege to be a part of the supervisory team.

Some of the chapters in the book draw upon papers that have appeared in various journals. In particular I am indebted to the *Journal of Property Research* for permission to reprint extracts and illustrations that first appeared as 'Towards an intelligent residential appraisal model' in 1999, vol. 16.

Any mistakes are entirely mine.

The Author

David Jenkins, BSc, MPhil, FRICS received his qualifications from the University of Reading in 1978 and the Polytechnic of Wales in 1992.

Since 1970 he has worked as a valuer in the private and public sectors, principally in the housing field. In 1987 he established a software consultancy and specialised in the development of software for valuation.

In 1994 David became a Fellow of the Society of Valuers and Auctioneers, and was appointed Halifax Research Fellow in Real Estate Appraisal at the University of Glamorgan 1995–6.

David is currently Senior Lecturer in Real Estate Appraisal at the University of Glamorgan, a part-time post, and is also a pastor of a church within the Baptist Union of Great Britain.

The author may be contacted through the publishers.

Chapter 1

Introduction

1.1 Residential valuation as a discipline

Residential valuation is the poor relation of professional appraisal practice.

To begin with there is no specific qualification or degree award for residential surveyors. Very little space has been devoted to the topic in UK higher and further education. The pre-eminent academic institutions train valuers in investment theory and techniques applicable to commercial property. Lesser institutions have developed portfolios of awards that are accredited by professional bodies like the newly merged Royal Institution of Chartered Surveyors (RICS) and Incorporated Society of Valuers and Auctioneers (ISVA). However, such awards are generally so broad in their compass that they rarely give more than passing consideration to specifically residential valuation issues. The consequence for practice is that new recruits into the profession invariably require significant on-the-job training, supervision and insurance cover.

Moreover, because of the substantial physical surveying input required by current residential appraisal practice, it is probable that a qualification as a building surveyor is at least as useful a starting point as a qualification in valuation specifically.

A similar picture emerges in relation to academic research. There is little by way of funding for explicitly residential appraisal research, nor is there a clear and specific mechanism for the promotion, management and dissemination of such material except within the broader category of surveying under the aegis of the RICS.

Commercially driven residential research has been a growth area in recent years. The chief stimulus to this growth has been the re-emergence of the residential property investment market. However, this research is better labelled residential market intelligence to distinguish it from appraisal theory, and relates to trends and opportunities for investment. Again, the commercial property equivalent dwarfs the residential sector.

In the conduct of professional affairs, as in academe, housing appraisal has only been half recognised as a distinct category. While there has been no housing division within the professional bodies, the establishment of a residential valuation committee within the RICS was testimony to an awareness of the distinctive role of the large numbers of residential surveyors. The new faculty structure for the RICS in which housing is expressly identified affords an opportunity to redress a long-standing imbalance.

Part of the explanation for the attitude to housing valuation is that researchers and practitioners alike see much greater complexity in commercial than in residential markets (see for example Connellan and James (1996)). Such views may be justified. Certainly, the markets for professional advice reflect or condition such views. Traditionally, rewards for appraisal personnel have been much higher in commercial than residential markets. Besides which, most RICS members and consumers do not believe that residential sales and letting agencies, which take the lion's share of residential activity, require professional qualification.

Nevertheless, residential appraisers are dealing with considerable complexity. First of all, housing is a complex commodity. At its most fundamental, the dwelling meets essential requirements for living: protection against climatic extremes, a place for activities preferably conducted under cover, a place for privacy and security, a place where physiological and psychological needs for territory are fulfilled. The dwelling will exhibit aspects of technological development in design and construction, often mediated through a regulatory framework. It will reflect communications technology in terms of its location and functionality. It will be an expression of the social needs and aspirations of individuals/family units and the groups to which they belong or with which they identify. As such, dwellings are polymorphous and heterogeneous. In appraisal parlance, all houses are unique.

Next, housing markets are undeniably complex. In Marshallian economics the forces of supply and demand determine house prices. Rational people individually making decisions to maximise their utility in aggregate produce a competitive general equilibrium (in all markets simultaneously). In a perfect market resources are used efficiently and no one could be better off without violating this Pareto-optimal allocation. This simplified model provides helpful insights into the derivation of value. In such a state, the value of a property newly arrived on the market could be deduced directly from analysis of the revealed prices (or rents) of comparable properties or equally directly computed from cost information.

It is safe to say, aside from Von Neuman's mathematical proofs that the conditions for a general equilibrium cannot exist (see Ormerod (1994) for a layman's guide), that none of the conditions of a perfect market begin to be met. The choice between value and cost information as the basis for a calculation becomes a pragmatic one: it concerns questions about the availability and reliability of data and its usefulness in the appraisal process in predicting value.

Viewed from the level of the typical transaction, the price of a dwelling is an expression of its value to two individual household units at a point in time, the vendor and the purchaser and their agents. This price may also reflect the interests of third parties, eg a moneylender or the tax authorities, the activities of other players in the marketplace whose signals have been interpreted by the parties, the agents acting for vendors of alternative properties, the unsuccessful bidders for the property sold and perceptions of general and local market conditions. The price will also reflect the state of other markets, markets for housing finance and finance more generally (assumed to be yet more unpredictable than housing markets – see Mueller (1995)), and substitute housing markets (non-owner-occupied housing) and factors which impact on such markets, eg forms of regulation and the degree of subsidy.

Furthermore, the value to the parties in a particular transaction may contain attributes to which every other purchaser may be indifferent. For example, environmental psychologists have analysed attachment to places, to neighbourhoods, towns and regions. Residential satisfaction is often tied to place attachment (Sundstrom *et al* 1996). What underpins this place attachment may not be clearly related to a measurable phenomenon of use in the comparison process, like proximity to a strong 'attractor', eg school provision or pleasant environment, the substance of quantitative economics.

Aggregate house price functions have difficulty representing such imponderables, but the individual purchaser is prepared to pay a premium to realise the aspiration. It is a component of effective demand, mediated through the house purchase process. The purchaser's own 'house price function' will reflect this factor, which may be measured by asking, 'How much are you prepared to pay to satisfy this want?'

Readers interested in further investigating the complexity of housing markets may wish to read the Miles (1994) text referred to in the bibliography at the end of this chapter. Essentially, residential valuation requires that techniques be deployed that are capable of satisfactorily assessing values of a heterogeneous product in a dynamic market.

Not only is the valuation problem non-trivial, but the owner-occupied sector of the residential property market is significant. The top 25 mortgage lenders in 1998 financed over 1.5 million transactions worth £89 billion (Source: Council of Mortgage Lenders). The total housing stock exceeds 24 million units, of which 67% are owner-occupied. The average value of an owner-occupied house is £90,000 (HMLR Residential Property Price Report, 1999). A crude valuation of the owner-occupied housing stock based on these statistics is £1,450 billion, while the value of the private rented sector is estimated at £150 billion. Forty per cent of all personal sector wealth is tied up in housing.

Such a large and dynamic market clearly impacts on the whole economic life of the nation. Housing and its value is not only an important discussion issue at the dining tables of the chattering classes, it regularly features in the deliberations of the Monetary Policy Committee of the Bank of England. The overheating of the housing market in the late 1980s and the subsequent collapse in asset values (1.7 million households experienced negative equity directly) had a direct and significant impact on labour mobility and, therefore, overall economic performance.

Naturally, such a painful phenomenon received considerable attention. Taxation policy in relation to owner-occupation was reversed. Controls for the regulation of mortgage lending and equity withdrawal were reviewed, albeit modestly. Restrictions in the main substitute market, the private rented sector, were removed. Latterly, the market mechanism for house selling has been investigated and attempts are being made to shorten the sale process and curtail gazumping. However, the market for the supply of valuation advice has not been scrutinised sufficiently.

This contrast between the importance of house price and the actual state of residential valuation as a discipline supplies one sub-text to this book. It might be anticipated that against such a backcloth there would be problems and tensions within residential valuation as a discipline. There have been. A serious examination of such issues is overdue.

1.2 Residential valuation theory

Perhaps the reason why so little theoretical consideration has been given to residential valuation is that the technique commonly used to value properties is rather simple to describe. Essentially a transaction is compared with earlier or concurrent transactions in similar properties, making allowances for differences revealed in the comparison process. Britton (1989), succinct as ever, points the finger to the nub of the problem when he states that while 'the method is simple in its general approach' it is 'dependent on considerable valuation judgement for its application.'

The simplicity of the technique and the complexity of the problem have produced in professionals a tendency to resist investigation so that the development of theory has been retarded. The research team at Glamorgan University can testify that this is true not only in the UK but in other countries where field investigations have been conducted (Malaysia, Europe and Australia). Nor is the field of residential valuation an isolated incident of this phenomenon.

The following quotation comes from Edward Wilson (1978: 176):

> Human beings require simple rules that solve complex problems. And they tend to resist any attempt to dissect the unconscious order and resolve of their daily lives. The principle has been expressed in psycho-analytic theory by Ernest Jones as follows: 'Whenever an individual considers a given (mental) process as being too obvious to permit of any investigation into its origin, and shows resistance to such an investig-ation, we are right in suspecting that the actual origin is concealed from him – almost certainly on account of its unacceptable nature.'

This book is written on the premise that residential appraisal practice is based on methods that are inherently unsatisfactory. Heuristics developed for residential valuation purposes are insufficient.

The comparative process is one of those basic simple stratagems that is capable of application across many disciplines. Happily, this means that theoretical progress occurring in any discipline may in the process of generalisation be applied to the domain under consideration.

In fact behavioural psychologists studying many different disciplines have developed a considerable body of theory in relation to the comparison process. The general conclusion must be that the process is fraught with difficulties. Subsequent academic effort applied within the real estate field confirms the general case (Issue Number 4, Volume 17, of the *Journal of Property Investment and Finance* celebrates the tenth anniversary of behavioural research in the discipline of property).

However, while behavioural psychology has usefully identified the lack of theoretical development in property appraisal, it has not been the only source of the development of theory. 'Economic psychology' has been concerned with measures of housing preference and choice and the relationship between them. Housing economics has focused on asset market approaches that have proven useful in predicting price movements, while a key thrust of real estate research has been on the development of new statistical models and on the transfer of new technologies into the domain. Some of these developments are aimed at supplanting the comparative approach while some aim to mitigate its weaknesses.

While it would be premature to suggest that an alternative to the comparative method is already available, it is reasonable to suggest that a sound critique of traditional methods can be elaborated and that much of the theoretical groundwork required for the development of new approaches has been completed.

1.3 Residential valuation practice

In the current residential sales process in the UK, the sale price is determined in two stages. In the first stage an asking price is established, usually by an estate agent. The initial formulation of asking price lacks precision. It is a 'ball park' figure.[1] This is not surprising because it is derived in a subjective manner, often without the input of professional advice,[2] in the knowledge that the 'market' will determine the actual sale figure in the second stage. Given the desire of sellers for a high price on sale and the optimism amid which asking prices are generated, agents may be tempted to inflate asking prices to encourage vendors to select their services (but, theoretically, not to the extent that agents gain a reputation for over-optimism).[3]

In the second stage the bid price is established and agreed between the parties. The second stage is concluded either by the cash offer of a purchaser (often relying on the asking price and no other professional advice) or by the valuation of a lender (73% of all property transactions in England and Wales are financed by mortgage according to HM Land Registry).

Professionally qualified personnel conduct this 'mortgage valuation' using the comparative process. They seek to establish the 'open market value' of the property as defined by the RICS.[4] This is a curious measure of value where the lender's real concern is future collateral to secure a loan.

As will be seen, this mortgage valuation process is compromised in practice not only by the drawbacks postulated in theory but also because all professional practice is conducted in the real world of relationships. For a valuation surveyor the context includes the fact that the lender is also the source of his or her livelihood. As Flyvberg (1998) has well demonstrated 'rationality is context-dependent' and 'the context of rationality is power'.

1.4 Book structure and research methods

Beyond this introduction, this book provides four substantive chapters, a concluding chapter and a technical appendix.

Chapter 2 reviews the traditional approach to the valuation of residential property. It is concerned with theory and practice. The theoretical review was dependent on a critique of literature principally from UK, American and Australian sources and an ongoing debate within the research team at Glamorgan. The practice review is drawn from contact with many practising valuers, primarily engaged in mortgage appraisal in the private sector. This contact has taken a variety of forms: consultancy work, observation, interviews and questionnaires. Furthermore, questionnaires have also been issued to and telephone interviews conducted with information technology managers in appropriate firms and institutions. In addition to a report funded by the ESRC (1996) this research has also provided material for six doctoral theses (five completed, one in progress) and two completed degrees of Master of Philosophy.

Chapter 3 is concerned with the supply of valuation advice. It attempts to build a case for the view that professional valuation advice to consumers should be independent. The opinions given here rely on information derived from the same sources and from case studies. However, all opinions are those of the author unless otherwise attributed.

The fourth chapter describes an alternative method for residential valuation and the development of prototype systems. This chapter draws on the experience of members of the research team in developing prototype valuation systems and providing consultancy to clients in the private and public sectors. Mathematical modelling and simulation techniques are employed that use both anonymously provided and publicly available data sets. Finally, the chapter draws on theoretical precepts and hypotheses that are described as appropriate.

Chapter 5 examines how valuation techniques are applied to the valuation of housing for public sector purposes, while the sixth chapter supplies a brief conclusion. A technical appendix describes some of the methods outlined in Chapter 4 in more detail.

Notes

1 In one case study of the sale of a property in a static market, four agents, all labelling themselves 'local', provided opinions of value that deviated by as much as 25% from the achieved sale price.
2 There is no requirement that estate agents be professionally qualified. Those who are often delegate the task of establishing asking prices to non-qualified personnel.
3 As with any other market, sellers' agents adopt different sales strategies. Some see their task as obtaining the best possible price for the client, which betrays a certain healthy self-interest where the fee is a percentage of the realised price. Others are prepared to adopt a strategy based on higher turnover, which usually means shorter market runs at more 'realistic' prices sometimes allied to flat fees. Needless to say, sellers themselves are rarely aware of these differences.
4 See *RICS Appraisal Valuation Manual*, PS4.2.

References and further reading

Britton, W., Davies, K. and Johnson, T. (1989) *Modern Methods of Valuation of Land, Houses and Buildings*, 8th edn. London: Estates Gazette.

Connellan, O.P. and James, H. (1996) *Estimated Realisation Price by Neural Networks*, Cutting Edge Conference. London: RICS.

Diaz, J. (ed.) (1999) 'Behavioural real estate analysis', *Journal of Property Investment and Finance*, 17(4).

Economic and Social Research Council (1996) *A Comparative Study of Residential Valuation Techniques and the Development of a House Value Model and Estimation System*. London: ESRC.

Flyvberg, B. (1998) *Rationality and Power: Democracy in Practice*. Chicago: University of Chicago Press..

Jenkins, D., Almond, N., Gronow, S., Lewis, O.M. and Ware, J. (1999) 'Towards an intelligent residential appraisal model', *Journal of Property Research*, 16(1), 67–90.

Miles, D. (1994) Housing, *Financial Markets and the Wider Economy*. Chichester: Wiley.

Mueller, G.R. (1995) 'Understanding real estate's physical and financial market cycles', *Real Estate Finance*, 12(3).

Ormerod, P. (1994) *The Death of Economics*. London and Boston: Faber & Faber.

Sundstrom, E., Bell, P.A., Busby, P.L. and Asmus, C. (1996) 'Environmental psychology', *Annual Review of Psychology*, 47, 485–512.

Wilson, E. (1978) *On Human Nature*. Cambridge, MA: Harvard University Press.

Chapter 2

Traditional Valuation Approach: Theory and Practice

2.1 Overview

In the United States the appraisal of open market value of a single family residence (SFR) proceeds using some average figure derived using three methods: the comparative method (comparable or market sales approach), the income (investment) method and the cost method. Even so the comparison process is still the most widely used in residential appraisal (Wolverton and Diaz, 1996).

In the UK, the majority of valuations for mortgage purposes are carried out by the comparative method alone, referred to as direct capital comparison (DCC) in this book. The alternative methods are briefly reported in the next section.

The comparative method is defined as:

> A method of valuation by which the rental or capital value of a property is assessed having regard to the prices or rents recently achieved by other properties which are similar in such matters as location, size, character and accessibility and the extent to which appropriate adjustments can be made to reflect differences. (Jones Lang Wooton and South Bank Polytechnic, 1989: 39)

As applied in the valuation of houses for sale in the open market, which comprise the vast majority of transactions in residential markets in the UK, the capital value obtained on sale is invariably the basis of comparison, hence the term direct capital comparison.

Valuers in the UK are prone to assume that methods used are correct, understood and sufficient, and consequently professionals and academics had devoted little attention to DCC. Within the UK, the principal text devoted to residential valuation, *The Valuation and Sale of Residential Property* by David Mackmin (1994), devotes just four pages to the comparative method while providing an excellent description of the residential sales and appraisal process. The most widely read general appraisal texts, such as Millington (1994) and Richmond (1994), devote five pages each to the comparative method.

11

By comparison, treatment of the method in texts beyond the UK is more extensive. For example, in the USA, the Appraisal Institute's *Appraising Residential Properties* (1994) devotes three chapters to the sales comparison approach. Nevertheless, there is the same assumption that the method is appropriate and sufficient given due diligence. This book challenges that basic assumption. DCC is a heuristic, a means of discovery. It may have been used more often in residential valuation than other traditional approaches like the investment method. However, this does not guarantee that it is sufficient. Is it more useful than the alternatives? In a 1996 report prepared with ESRC funding, the Glamorgan team suggested that in the face of the market collapse of 1988–9, DCC broke down and that its usefulness took a considerable period to re-establish (see Gronow *et al* 1996).

This chapter is concerned to describe DCC, its strengths and weaknesses, from both theoretical and practical points of view, but first a brief section looks at alternative traditional methods available to but rarely used in the context of residential valuation by valuers in the UK.

2.2 Traditional alternatives to comparative analysis

Theoretically, the valuer has a number of alternative methods at his or her disposal in the valuation of residential property: the income approach, the cost-based approach and the residual method.

In the UK, the income approach to valuation is most commonly used in the valuation of commercial property, where the property is seen as an investment and value is based on the net income it produces. This income is capitalised by a factor representing growth, operating expenses, liquidity and risk (Baum and Crosby, 1995). A simplified example of this approach might be as follows:

Rent	$£x$
Less Outgoings	$£y$
Net income	$£(x - y)$
Capitalisation factor	z
Value	$£z(x - y)$

(The above is a deliberately simplified example which ignores lease structures involving, for example, varying rental levels and reversionary interests.)

As applied to residential property, the method is also complicated by the need to take into account legislative factors. A number of texts treat this approach as applied to residential property investment (see Rees, 1992; Baum and Sams, 1997; Britton *et al* 1989), though a number of changes have occurred in the legislation affecting residential property in recent years that have not yet been satisfactorily dealt with in textbooks.[1]

Within the UK the majority of housing is for owner-occupation, historically with only some 7% of the housing stock in the private rented sector. Information on rents and capitalisation rates in the market has therefore been poor in comparison with the number of available sales in the owner-occupied sector. Consequently, unless the property is an investment, the DCC approach is used in preference and very little cross-sector analysis is conducted.

An argument can be constructed in favour of the use of such rental evidence as is available in capital valuations. In this argument, the net income, which is received as rent, is equated to the monthly servicing cost of a loan to purchase the property plus a profit element. This monthly cost could then be capitalised at an appropriate interest rate.

The cost approach, also known as the contractor's test, is a method used where a property is seldom let or sold and for which therefore there is neither evidence of rental nor capital values. This type of valuation is commonly associated with the valuation of public buildings, for example schools, universities and libraries, and particularly in rating cases, and therefore this approach is rarely used in valuing residential properties.

Millington (1994) provides a simplified outline of the calculation used, as follows:

	Cost of site
Plus	Cost of buildings
Less	Depreciation allowance
And	Obsolescence allowance
	Value of existing property

More detailed accounts of the method can be seen in a number of rating cases, for example *Dawkins (VO)* v *Royal Leamington Spa Corporation* (1961)[2] and *Gilmore (VO)* v *Baker-Carr* (1963).[3] In rating cases it has been suggested that the cost-based approach should be adopted as a 'last resort'. This is largely because the basis of valuation is open market value and cost and value are not equal, save in perfect markets. Nevertheless, cost information may be useful where confidence is low in the application of other approaches and a reasonable argument in favour of a cost-based approach can be constructed (see for example Hendershott, 1994).

A more widely used approach in the valuation of residential property is the residual approach. However, this approach is only relevant where a property has development or redevelopment potential. Millington (1994) cites a simplified example in which a property currently worth £50,000 having £20,000 worth of expenditure carried out for improvements could sell for £90,000, the latent value (of £20,000) being released by expenditure on improvements. Darlow (1988) provides a comprehensive overview of the residual method that he suggests can be simplified into the following type of equation:

	Sale price of completed development		A
less	Cost of development	B	
	Profit allowance	C	B + C
equals	Residue for purchasing land/property		D
	ie D = A – (B + C)		

2.3 Comparative analysis

The comparative process is at the heart of much decision-making. Economists talk in terms of maximising utility or optimising resource allocation. Other social scientists have derived different measures of satisfaction or preference. In countless pursuits human beings have developed performance criteria to assist in terms of ranking or choosing between alternatives and in formulating bids. However they are measured, some form of comparison is often the only way to choose between preferences.

In the simplest case, the choice is between alternatives having a single attribute. More commonly the choice is between alternatives that are complex, that is to say each option has many attributes.

Apparently, when selecting somewhere to live, many people first draw up a list of the attributes that if realised in the purchase would maximise satisfaction. This represents a rational approach to decision-making. However, within the bounds of this rational approach it is conceivable that considerations other than the satisfaction of detailed aspirations in regard to the property may apply. Rational purchasers might entertain a trade-off between, for example, satisfying aspirations of the property and minimising search time and cost (or meeting a deadline to acquire a particularly attractive financial product). Rational purchasers also

Attribute	1 Acacia Avenue	3 Larch Crescent	5 Douglas Fir Bank
Bungalow	✓	✓	✓
Detached	✓	✗	✓
Private	✓	✓	✗
3 beds	✓	✓	✓
Near mum and dad	✗	✓	Too near

Figure 2.1 A preference list for choosing between alternative properties

include investors and speculators for whom the detailed attributes of property may have minimal significance.

Aside from these considerations, purchasers are known not to approach the decision in a completely rational way. There is an emotional aspect to any housing transaction and a trade-off between satisfying preferences and minimising emotional strain may be postulated.

However, let us assume that many purchasers construct an attribute list. First attempts may be idealised – they are not yet informed by constraints that will apply, like availability and cost. Revised lists will take into account experience gained in attempting to satisfy first preferences. Ultimately such lists may be refined as consumers move from preferences to choices. The comparative process is iterative and dynamic.

Each item in a preference list represents an attribute that people value. Sometimes the list is used as the basis for a comparison grid like that shown in Figure 2.1. This allows the decision-makers to bring all the information together. If the attributes are ranked in order of importance, in the example the anticipated choice will be 1 Acacia Avenue, assuming that price is not a factor.

Of course, the grid could be far more sophisticated. Each of the attributes (rows) might contain a scale of points rather than ticks to show the extent to which each attribute is satisfied. The final choice may then relate to the highest points total for each property (column). Furthermore, each attribute may be weighted as well as ranked. For instance, the 'bungalow' attribute may be 'considerably' more important than the 'private' attribute. If the term 'considerably' could be evaluated, then numerical weights may be attached to each attribute (row). The total would then relate to the product of points and weights.

Such a points system may be somewhat arbitrary and introduce a flavour of spurious accuracy. A further refinement of a system would permit ranges of points for each attribute and assign subjective probabilities across the ranges, ie to use 'fuzzy' instead of 'crisp' numbers. The simple grid would have become a 'fuzzy' spreadsheet. In fact, there are software products designed to do just this, eg Fuzicalc™. Of course, it would be far more anthropomorphic to use terms like 'considerably' to measure importance than ranges of numbers, so a final refinement would be to label ranges appropriately.

The whole point of the approach is to assist the purchaser(s) to decide. Ultimately their preferences, however calculated, will be translated into a bid expressed in money terms. A successful bid becomes a transaction price.

The valuer's task is analogous to the process described with one major difference. The valuer is concerned not with an individual's preferences but with some expression of social preferences. The reasons why this is the case may require explanation.

Most residences are bought with borrowed money. Lenders have an obligation to be prudent; they are therefore concerned with the security of a property as an investment. Objectively they are not keen to lend more money against the property as security than is likely to be realised on sale at some future date. The lender would wish to discount any bid that failed this test. The market has a means of dealing with 'underbids'. They tend to be eliminated by higher bids.[4] But if the highest bid is too high, left to its own devices the market has no means of dealing with it except to leave the bidder or the bidder's lender to live with the consequences (*caveat emptor*).

Valuation is a traditional means by which the lender assesses whether a bid is an overbid. The bid is assessed in relation to other previous successful or contemporary bids. (The other means by which lenders deal with an overbid is to ensure that the bidder endures the consequences.) In a cash economy, without lenders or borrowers, some form of valuation analysis would still be conducted directly for the prudent purchaser, who is assumed to be self-interested and wants value for money.

So valuers are concerned with a measure that expresses social preferences. In the context of mortgage lending the measure of value should reflect the sustainability of the bid in terms of the security and the market in which it is traded. The question is how to construct that measure of social preferences.

Theoretically, it should be possible to elicit the preference lists of many purchasers and aggregate them. On reflection, however, this may not be so easy. Not only are there many attributes of a property that require listing, but different individuals will rank and weight attributes differently. They may also switch rankings and weightings in response to different situations (though this latter problem is not too worrisome given that a measure of social preference always needs to be applied specifically). Certainly, to construct and maintain a preference measure and apply it would require a great deal of effort, not least intellectual effort, in constructing a sampling strategy.

Alternatively, it should be possible to develop an objective measure of property attributes. Indeed, since the 1970s there have been many hedonic price index studies that have attempted to estimate implicit prices for individual property attributes. These also require a considerable effort and are not problem-free (Maclennan, 1982).

It can be concluded that the objectification of such subjective judgements is an inherently complex process. However, it is a process that actually occurs, albeit in a form removed from the theoretical model, ie housing markets.

Given that preferences are translated into bid and transaction prices, it is far easier to start with such data. In comparative analysis, the valuer's task becomes the 'inverse' of the process summarised in Figure 2.1. Known prices of comparable properties are analysed in terms of their attributes. Theoretically, this analysis should encompass every attribute of a transaction that was different from every other attribute in selected comparable transactions.

This is not to say that valuers ever elicit a preference or attribute list from a purchaser. Nor do valuers share with other valuers preference lists that they have constructed for the sake of consistency or to aid in the comparative process. There are no standards in this process. Valuers approach the problem entirely subjectively. Hence the notion that valuation is an art not a science.

It was noted above that textbooks tend to assume that DCC is a sufficient methodology. Consequently textbooks are not rich in theory. Instead they tend to rationalise or idealise practice and leapfrog those aspects of cognitive theory that relate to human problem-solving and that identify potential methodological weaknesses. It is commonly suggested that valuation by DCC can be broken down into four steps. In Mackmin's (1994) words:

1 Select comparables
2 Extract, confirm and analyse comparable sale prices.
3 Adjust sale prices for noted differences.
4 Formulate an opinion of open market value for subject property.

This schema is a rationalisation of observed practice and provides a useful framework for a critical review, though for the purpose of this analysis three steps are described:

1 selection of comparables;
2 analysis of comparables;
3 formulation of an opinion of value.

Theoretically valuers are presumed to follow this sequence in practice and each step is discrete. According to most commentators the formulation of an opinion of open market value for the subject property is the final stage in the process. From observations recorded by the research team, it became clear that valuers are much more pragmatic and that, for example, their formulation of opinion can occur at any point in the process.

   In practice it appears that this point is reached when valuers are sufficiently confident in an opinion. Once they have sufficient evidence to justify the opinion they stop 'experimenting'. The answer may not be 'correct' but it is sufficient within the parameters of the problem. These parameters include not only the technical, but also the contextual – the social, political and economic – as well the 'complex array of routines, expectations, roles, norms, axioms and unwritten rules that make up the practitioner's everyday world' (James, 1997). For the valuer they include the size of the caseload, the amount of the fee, the lender's need to secure the business, the practitioner's position in the company, the availability of evidence, etc.

   In the following sections each of the three steps is considered in context.

2.4 Selection of comparables

Theoretically, the selection of comparables requires the valuer to identify the most useful transactions that will provide evidence to deduce an opinion of value. American and UK literature describes two alternative strategies for comparable selection. The first is the selection of sufficient comparables which, after adjustment, will provide the valuer with a range of values within which, *ceteris paribus*, the value of the subject property is presumed to lie. The second strategy involves the selection of a single property (or more correctly transaction) record that can be regarded as making a matching pair with the subject property, after suitable 'adjustment'.

The number of comparables selected for the first strategy will depend on the circumstances. Various commentators suggest a minimum of three, though in the UK this would appear to be a maximum in practice.

In the United States the Federal National Mortgage Association (FNMA) requires three comparables as a minimum while four or five comparables are usually cited for MAI (Member of the Appraisal Institute) analysis, 'although there is no absolute requirement for this' (Frampton, 1994).

Clearly, the more comparables that are available to the valuer, the better position the valuer is in to substantiate the valuation. In practice, the problem has been finding at least some evidence of similar transactions and bringing skill to bear.

The second strategy, identification of a single matching pair, appears to be fraught with dangers. For example, if Mr Inglett buys his house primarily in order to live near a relative, then his preference list will reflect this. This may well influence the price that he pays. A valuer would need to know this if relying on Mr Inglett's transaction as a matching pair to Mr Jarero's purchase of a neighbouring property. If not, then Mr Jarero may be paying a premium to live near Mr Inglett's relative.

A valuer using such evidence would need to research the matching pair transaction in some detail and provide a full description of the approach adopted and information used in forming an opinion. Clearly if transactions are identical, there is a good case to be made for the adoption of this approach in the absence of other evidence in stable markets.

However, in addition to the two reported strategies, the following strategy has also been observed. Valuers sometimes use a series of matching pair approaches. Rather than use the comparison grid – which can become arbitrary – they seem to follow a strategy that can be labelled 'complex matching'.

One part of that strategy – though not obligatory – is to identify ceiling and floor values above or below which the valuer infers that the value cannot lie. As each new comparable transaction is analysed, it is matched first with the ceiling and floor comparables. Analysis of the transaction yields one of three potential outcomes:

- It might establish a new ceiling or floor value.
- It may be eliminated because, being dissimilar in some regard, the value it suggests is in excess of/below the previously established ceiling/floor.
- It may be retained for further analysis being sufficiently similar and within the ceiling/floor range.

Whether or not the ceiling/floor approach is taken, the transactions are matched as pairs to establish a ranking – the most useful comparable is highest in the order and so on. This may suggest more precision than is actually the case – the ranking may be somewhat fuzzy. Below a certain threshold comparables that appeared to be useful may now be eliminated in favour of those of higher rank.

It is noticeable that sometimes transactions are used only to facilitate partial comparison. For example, a value for an attribute of the subject property may be inferred by analysis of two other properties that are alike in all respects except the attribute under consideration. This suggests a value for the attribute that may be used in the valuation of the subject even though neither of the other properties is sufficiently similar to make the highest ranks of comparables.

Each of the chosen transactions is then compared in turn with the subject property in more detail (though this part of the process may be completed using the grid). The process cuts the complexity into manageable chunks.

As well as a search s*trategy*, the selection process requires search *criteria*: key attributes that are used to select comparables with relevant qualities. In the case of a matching pair, most textbooks suggest that the 'match' is likely to be a property within the same street or estate, suggesting that the search criteria will be spatial. Some commentators suggest that valuers may use data from a wider geographic area. Indeed where there are no similar properties in the same geographic area, valuers are observed to look to similar properties in a similar or near geographic area.

Location is important not in itself but because of its specific attributes. Residential location theory started with the premise that utility was a function of accessibility to a central business district. In classical 'trade-off' theory, the sole determinant of location rent was transport-saving costs. But in residential choice, accessibility is important not only in relation to work, but also in relation to the whole gamut of social activity.

Environmental externalities and neighbourhood preferences are all reflected in house prices. Perhaps search criteria should embrace 'bundles' of such attributes explicitly rather than simply use location as a surrogate. Databases of neighbourhood indicators have been used in the UK and are more prevalent in the US.

If literature emphasises 'location, location, location'[5] as the search criteria, perhaps a more precise formulation would be 'segment, segment, segment' because markets are often differentiated by non-spatial attributes according to the functional requirements of purchasers. In other words, preference lists do not always rank 'location' attributes first.

Whatever the search strategy or criteria it is axiomatic that the comparable(s) selected should be consistent with the observations that have been reported for the subject. The selected transactions must be similar, but what constitutes 'similar' is nowhere defined. Very early on in the research programme, valuers in Cardiff were observed to use several 'critical' attributes of a dwelling repeatedly in imputing a 'base' value. These same attributes are invariably included in valuation regression studies.

Experienced valuers' knowledge of an area is such that they may dispense with a formal search of the comparable register or database and select transactions from memory directly for inclusion in the comparable list. Like the experienced chess player, common configurations of attributes are retained as single perceptual units, many bits of information stored in more manageable chunks. This process is facilitated by the recollection of 'labels' for different styles of house, builders' names or periods of construction, and further facilitated by associations: particular styles of property are remembered in association with common defects or neighbourhood characteristics.

One unsatisfactory means of describing the process is that the valuers operate with a number of indices: a spatial index, a building form index and so on, which they use to rapidly select comparable properties. The advantage of this description is that systems analysts may then replicate this behaviour approximately within databases

Experienced valuers also appear to look for and remember transactions which are representative of a class of properties. Valuers are observed to use a 'good' comparable repeatedly.

Valuers with access to copious data and modern database management tools have the facility to search on multiple criteria (though the typical searches encountered are location or property type first together with measures of accommodation and price range). Where many comparables are revealed, choosing the most recent is balanced against choosing those most 'closely comparable', though this latter expression is another form of 'similar' and lacks definition.

In the mid-1990s the research team at Glamorgan developed a search engine that trawls through data recursively and selects the most closely matching comparables by multiple attributes (a brief description of the processes is included in section 4.2). A prototype of this software was made available as a Microsoft Access database with a free run-time licence. At the time, very few people responded to the opportunity to acquire it confirming survey questionnaire studies that most firms lacked even elementary database tools and concepts.

One of the considerations in comparable selection is confidence in the transaction evidence. The source of the information, its validation and the completeness of the transaction data certainly influence the decision to select the comparable. While valuers do remember 'good' comparables, the consistent use of the best quality information within a database requires that the database contains fields to record transaction quality.

One of the difficulties facing valuers in the aftermath of a peak or trough is the dearth of transactions as the market goes through the phase of 'wait and see'. Comparable selection exhibits unusual characteristics in such a period, including a very weak form of time series analysis. The process is described as follows: a particular transaction is useful – most of the attributes are known; there is nothing that renders this transaction exceptional. Furthermore, there are earlier comparables with high degrees of similarity. The comparable 'set', the earlier and current transactions taken together, is indicative of market movement. If the comparable set is thought to be representative of market movement, it is thought to be appropriate as evidence elsewhere. Use as a comparable is generalised and the 'set' is frequently selected. A weaker version of this process may occur in mid-cycle.

An analogous process also occurs when valuers are asked to undertake appraisals outside their normal sphere of activity. As Jenkins and Gronow (1990) observed, experienced valuers seem to develop a 'value structure' for the markets in which they operate. When operating in markets new to them, they are able to use scraps of transaction evidence from the new environment that will enable them to recalibrate a 'value structure' that can then be applied. However, it may take many months (and transactions) before sufficient local knowledge is acquired to appraise competently. Almond (1999) has conducted detailed research into such competence and suggests that a system of local licensing is appropriate.

Having found the comparables, Shenkel (1978) notes that checks should be made to remove any unrepresentative or non-bona fide sales from this selection. Essentially, provided the comparable sale price is that of one in the open market, or unless a 'single overriding factor' (Dennett, 1997: 51) is present,[6] then it will be acceptable. Consequently if the circumstances of the sale suggest a premium or discount to open market value, eg a purchaser paid 'under market value' because of the vendor's need for an urgent sale, the evidence of the transaction should be disregarded. While this is clear enough, it does not help in solving the difficulty of identifying when this constraint applies, for unless the transaction record identifies the problem the valuer will need to rely on memory.

Historically, search criteria have been quite limited and comparable evidence has been chosen because it is thought to be directly relevant to a transaction. But if more and better quality socio-economic data becomes available and modelling of the underlying structure of markets is enhanced, it seems likely that the legitimate field of search for comparable evidence would broaden and better use be made of evidence that may once have been considered marginal.

In the event of there being no comparables, DCC is not possible. In such circumstances a valuation will have to be made based on some informed opinion (and so stated in the report to the client), perhaps utilising one of the alternative valuation approaches described earlier.

2.5 Analysis of comparables

Most texts suggest that once the comparables have been selected, adjustments are required for any noted differences using a 'sales comparison grid', a simple spreadsheet. An example of such a grid is shown in Figure 2.2. Again the attributes of the transactions are contained in rows, the columns containing the properties to be compared.

Where one of the comparable properties has an extra bedroom, this is denoted in the first column and a cost or value adjustment is

Comparables ⇒ Attributes ⇓	1 Acacia Avenue	3 Larch Crescent	5 Douglas Fir Bank	7 Idle Way
Price sold (£) Date of sale	51,000 30/3/00	50,000 22/5/00	52,000 7/7/00	51,000 12/4/00
Adjusting factors:				
No. beds	–	1 extra –£3,000	–	–
Reception rooms	–	–	–	–
Kitchen	–	–	–	–
Bathroom	–	–	–	–
WC	–	1 extra –£1,500	–	–
Central heating	–	–	–	–
Double glazing	–	–	–	Yes –£2,750
Garage	–	–	–	–
Condition	–	–	£4,000	–
Location	–	–	–	–£1,250
Planning	–	–	–	–
Adjusted value (£)	51,000	45,500	48,000	47,000

Figure 2.2 Typical comparable adjustment sheet or comparison grid

made in the second column (in this case a deduction of £3,000 to reflect one extra bedroom). An alternative to monetary adjustments has been observed, in which percentage allowances are made to the comparable properties using the same basic process. Refinements that would incorporate subjective probability are also possible using fuzzy spreadsheet software.

Several commentators suggest that the measure used in the process should be value rather than cost and note that, in practice, where this approach is taken, these measures are usually heuristically assigned. Nevertheless cost is advantageous given that on-line digests of building costs are readily available to reflect, for example, differences in accommodation. According to Adair and McGreal (1987) 'theoretical and empirical studies have shown that average attribute prices for a group of houses can be determined using multiple regression analysis', suggesting that adjustments may be quantified using such techniques.

Textbook examples (and those encountered in practice) tend to limit the adjusting factors to property and not transaction attributes. This means that all the non-property influences on transaction price are omitted from explicit analysis and are subsumed in the 'final' step of formulating an opinion of value.

One of the Glamorgan research team, Dr Nigel Almond, was particularly interested in how attributes are classified. He noted (Almond, 1999) that, in making adjustments for differences, the various commentators offered quite different classifications. Thus Mackmin (1994) defines three main classes to include sales conditions along with location and 'condition and accommodation', while noting too the importance of time in the analysis. Adair (1992) offers property, distance, environment and finance; Greaves (1984) noted the physical property, immediate physical amenities, location in terms of time and distance, location in terms of neighbourhood, and finance; Reynolds (1984) noted date, location, motivation, physical similarity and encumbrances; Britton notes only two, those of accommodation and situation; the *RICS Appraisal and Valuation Manual* (Annex to Guidance Note 3) (RICS, 1995) includes classes for property type and accommodation, exterior, interior, services, defects and potential defects, locality, amenities and encumbrances. Attribute classification is not really central to the discussion here but section 2.8 below discusses the issue in a little more detail.

Beyond classes of variables are the variables themselves. Of particular importance was a study in the UK by Adair (1992) which defined the major characteristics that impact on value (from both the valuer and the consumer) across different markets in an area of East Belfast. Overall a composite set of 47 attributes were defined. Jenkins (1992) identifies 69 variables in use by the valuers observed in that study. The *RICS Appraisal and Valuation Manual* (Annex to Guidance Note 3) (RICS, 1995) lists some sixty attributes within its classification which could have some impact on value, including a number of attributes which are really sub-classes which may be further expanded.

There is an unhelpful emphasis on supply-related variables in UK real estate appraisal literature and professional guidance notes on DCC and this is reflected in UK real estate practice. It may be that the adjustment grid is not the appropriate place to treat demand-side factors. If so it may be expected that they would be treated independently in the analysis or else as part of the 'final' step in the process, the formulation of opinion. As shall be seen, there is usually no explicit treatment of these attributes at all, though clearly market price is determined by supply and demand.

This is not to suggest that commentators are unaware of the importance of economic factors. Mackmin (1994) devotes a chapter section to the market. Millington (1994) offers a whole, if short, chapter. But it may be more useful to turn to theoretical and applied economic texts in order to identify and classify demand-side attributes which impact on value.

For example, Waxman and Lenard (1994), in a book devoted to the description of the Australian residential market, allocate a substantial chapter to a consideration of the characteristics of demand for residential property. They identify, *inter alia*, population growth and age structure, household formation rates, migration in various forms, income levels, cost and availability of housing finance, government subsidies and incentives, lifestyles and attitudes. Compelling logic suggests that there needs to be a place for analysing such attributes in any decision on residential value.

Of course, not only commentators but also practitioners are aware of the impact of demand factors on markets. Subsequent (prior?) to the treatment of physical factors, during which demand is theoretically assumed to be constant, explicit analysis of demand factors should occur. The observed absence of such treatment gives cause for alarm.

Having identified the attributes, two further difficulties need to be considered in the analysis of comparables: time and the quantum of adjustment.

2.5.1 *The treatment of time in the analysis of comparables*

Commentators often treat the question of 'time' separately in the adjustment process. Clearly, the more time that has elapsed between the valuation dates of the subject and comparable properties, the more the usefulness of the comparable transaction decreases. In this respect, a number of organisations in the US provide guidelines suggesting that comparables should be sales completed within the past twelve months, with one organisation requiring sales that were completed in the previous six months.

Clearly valuers should make reference to available time series data such as published house price indices. The Halifax and Nationwide house price indices have been considered as strong authority for measuring the performance of the housing market (Antwi, 1995), though caution is required. Commentators have reported differential movements of the indices in the same periods (see for example Eade, 1995). In recent years criticism has been levelled at these two indices and it may be that HM Land Registry's house price bulletin, derived from all transaction data, will supplant them.

In any event, there is little evidence of the systematic use of such indices in the valuation process in the UK. The software described in section 4.2 addresses this deficiency by offering an option that automatically smoothes data for movements in indices.

Even so, such indices cannot be definitive in view of the highly fragmented nature of housing markets. Jamieson (1996) considers the potential use of such indices as limited given the difference in prices within regions. Indeed there is evidence for the view that markets are highly fragmented, containing 'hot and cold' spots. In such circumstances, average is a statistical fiction.

In addition to general market cycles, sub-markets may also display independent cyclical behaviour, and are in any case prone to volatility arising from significant economic events that impact on local or sub-regional markets. Valuers react to such phenomena subjectively. Throughout the research period the team encountered only one local index constructed by a firm of chartered surveyors.

2.5.2 *The quantum of adjustment*

The other area of difficulty is the quantum of adjustment that is to be made in reflecting attribute differences. For example, proximity to an environmental attribute regarded as a nuisance may have a negative effect on value. In the marketplace, some potential buyers will be more influenced by this attribute than others and will discount their offer more deeply. *Ceteris paribus*, the property will be sold to the individual who is least perturbed by its presence. This suggests that the valuer will always be correct to choose the least discount in respect of any such attribute (especially where demand is tending to outstrip supply). It would be interesting to measure this effect. Does the valuer's adjustment truly reflect this behaviour? Does the adjustment tend to the mean or is the valuer perhaps simply imposing his or her own values in the process? Similarly, some attributes, eg a church, a bus stop, a railway terminal, have a negative impact for some potential purchasers and a positive impact for others (degree of proximity is one issue here). How do valuers deal with this ambiguity? Is it ignored? Is the positive aspect measured? Or, again, is it the valuer's subjective view that emerges? In these instances, there is no common approach or guidance to valuers, but the factors that might influence the valuer's subjective view need to be considered.

It would be surprising if no bias crept into the valuer's judgement on account of his or her gender. A nationwide survey conducted by Knight Frank in 1996 in conjunction with *Ideal Home* magazine questioned country house buyers as to what features made them choose one property against another, ignoring obvious factors like location, position and style. Particular attention was given to the differences between gender and the results produced quite different priorities. In so far as valuers have assimilated these preferences in this market sector, it might be expected that they would award a premium to those properties that possessed these attributes.

In so far as valuers shared these preferences, it might be expected that male and female valuers would rank attributes in different order in terms of their impact on value, and attach different measures of value in the adjustment process.

Similar observations would apply to the social class of the valuer, ie values are adjusted through a middle-class lens and there may be a potential incapacity to appreciate important aspects of the house purchase decision for household units at remote ends of the social scale. Ethnic origin, marital status and beliefs are also likely to have an influence on such judgements.

There is no evidence that valuers use confidence factors in relation to attribute information. Given the high incidence of missing or uncertain data that is engendered by the way in which comparables data is managed, there are the further dangers that decisions are reached based on wrong data and, perhaps more significantly, decisions are made without properly considering the effects of uncertainty. Off-the-shelf software for representing uncertain numbers is available at modest prices. Such software is capable of accepting ranges of values with confidence or belief factors associated with each value in the range. The calculation outcome is a belief graph that contains all possible outcomes from the uncertain input. The highest point of the belief graph represents the value thought most likely.

Care is still required because anchoring and other effects are present (see section 2.6 for a description). Research by Alpert and Raiffa (see Kahneman *et al* 1982), among others, shows that in constructing subjective probability distributions, experts attach greater certainty over too narrow confidence intervals than their knowledge warrants. This concern is academic given that no surveying firm encountered employed such techniques.

In the absence of sufficient data, if the comparable selection process is problematic, the adjustment process may be considered as arbitrary. It relies on 'skilful performances'. However, it seems that valuers are shy when it comes to maintaining records of this skill. Indeed, from observations, it is clear that adjustment grids and a formal adjustment process were customarily absent even when data was available. This is not to say that there was no adjustment process at all; rather the suggested method, the 'comparison grid', universally employed in the US, is often ignored in practice in the UK.

In practice, valuers dispense with an explicit comparable grid though the process (or one of its variants) may be carried out mentally. Clearly mental comparisons of all of the attributes even on a limited sample are not possible. What appears to happen is a filtration process: the more useful comparables have already been selected, the valuer now focuses not on the attributes that are similar but on the major dissimilarities. The adjustment grid is collapsed to a few significant attributes which affect value and either an arithmetic or fuzzy calculation sums positive and negative effects to provide a total adjustment figure, or else each of the adjustments is in turn applied to the 'starting' figure directly.

The dangers are that some of the attributes (hopefully less important ones) are missed or that mistakes are made in the calculation. The problem in disputed cases is that the mechanics of this process are not usually recorded. The 'judgement' is not reported explicitly though it may have been made explicitly, the lack of a report reflecting that deep-seated lack of belief in the probity of the process.

To address these problems, valuation systems developed by Glamorgan rendered this process explicit, thereby guaranteeing that commercially they would fail!

2.6 Formulation of an opinion of value

This is a critical moment in the decision process yet literature is at its most sparse here. Mackmin (1994: 387) notes that valuers in the UK are 'reluctant to explain how they analyse and how they value by direct sales comparison'. Scott (1988) and Jenkins (1992) noted in studies of appraisal decision-makers that, though they were competent, they were nonetheless unable to articulate their full decision process.

Schön (1991: 50) suggests that this is a general phenomenon of professional decision-making:

> In his day-to-day practice [the professional] makes innumerable judgements of quality for which he cannot state adequate criteria, and he displays skills for which he cannot state the rules and procedures. Even when he makes conscious use of research-based theories and techniques, he is dependent on tacit recognitions, judgements, and skilful performances.

Even so he noted that this is not an unthinking approach:

> On the other hand, both ordinary people and professional practitioners often think about what they are doing, sometimes even while doing it. Stimulated by surprise, they turn thought back on action and on the knowing which is implicit in the action.

And he concluded:

> It is this entire process of reflection-in-action which is central to the 'art' by which practitioners sometimes deal well with situations of uncertainty, instability, uniqueness and value conflict.

From this perspective, professional decision-making may be viewed as a form of experimentation, which is less rigorous than controlled experiment yet valid within the confines of the problem parameters. Schön describes how professionals develop a repertoire that is more subtle and flexible than the sum of case knowledge derived from practical experience.

Given the importance of the agent in this process – the valuer –

this leads to anticipation that professional experience will be a key consideration in the formulation of opinion. Indeed Adair and McGreal (1995) indicate that valuers themselves 'stress the importance of experience in the market place'.

Scott (1988) pointed to the different heuristics of the newly qualified para-professional in comparison with a skilled colleague. Cognitive theory provides an explanation. With experience comes a subtle change in the heuristics deployed which is observable across disciplines. Means–end analysis exhibited by novices is, with experience, replaced by the application of compiled knowledge (Stillings *et al* 1995). Semantic networks are enriched by experience and experts manipulate 'chunks' of information which speed performance (Czernkowski, 1990). This suggests that experienced professionals will:

- come sooner in the process to the formulation of an opinion;
- more readily identify the exceptional case;
- minimise analysis, at least explicit analysis; and
- select evidence to test or justify their opinion.

Whether or not the valuer is experienced, a heuristic called 'anchoring and adjustment' is commonly found in this process (Jenkins, 1992; Gallimore, 1994). Tversky and Kahneman (1974: 1128) describe this heuristic as follows: 'People make estimates by starting from an initial value that is adjusted to yield the final answer.' This may well be an iterative process in which the starting value is refined in the light of all the evidence. The discussion of experience suggests that iterations will be fewer for the mature professional whose initial starting figure will be closer to the final opinion. This all seems innocent enough, but the process contains hidden dangers that bias the outcome as the mind deceives itself.

Slovic and Lichtenstein (1971) originally demonstrated that even when given quite arbitrary starting values, adjustments are rarely sufficient and biased towards the starting figure. That means that there is a tendency to discount evidence encountered in the analysis. Perhaps professionals prize intuitive opinions too highly.

The starting figure or range may be a fuzzy computation based on general experience, or it may be deduced more explicitly from comparison data. In these processes, two further heuristics are encountered, availability and representativeness.

Valuers may estimate the frequency of transactions in a class, or the likelihood that a transaction is valid by the ease of recall – referred to as availability – of transactions. It has already been observed above that valuers use 'good' evidence repeatedly and indeed this is seen as a virtue. Tversky and Kahneman (1974) demonstrated that, while this estimation procedure is valuable, it results in systematic errors.

Valuers rely on comparing a current transaction with other known transactions, ie past transactions representative or similar to it. In relying on past transactions, other factors that should affect the judgement are ignored. Kahneman *et al* (1982) detail insensitivity to prior probability, predictability and sample size, illusions of validity and misconceptions of regression as biases in this representativeness heuristic. Readers wishing to explore these problems in more detail are referred to that text, which gives copious illustrative examples along with a number of experiments to demonstrate bias magnitudes.

The initial opinion of value, the selection of evidence to test it, the analysis of that evidence and the final formulation of opinion are all potentially biased. These biases infect the whole valuation process even when starting from an arbitrary figure.

However, in practice, valuers rarely start from an arbitrary figure. In the UK, the research uncovered a real danger. The proposed transaction price (agreed between vendor and purchaser and awaiting validation by the lender) is substituted for an arbitrary initial value. The figure is especially compelling where there may be little other evidence on which to formulate an opinion. Given that the transaction price is generally revealed to the valuer[7] prior to his or her decision, real distortion may occur in this process. In the US Wolverton and Diaz (1996) detected a biasing effect in the selection of comparables when valuers are provided with a copy of the sale price. The Glamorgan team hypothesised that a similar effect is also present during analysis whereby adjustments to comparable data are 'weighted' in order to support this 'target' figure, thereby compounding the problem.

The overall effect has been identified in the UK where, in an analysis of over 100,000 transactions, 68% of valuation decisions matched the transaction price (agreed subject to confirmation) to the exact pound, while 90% of valuations fell within 5% of this figure. How likely is it that such precision would exist if valuers were following one of the theoretical approaches described above?

There is a fine distinction between analysing evidence to test or to justify an opinion. But there is a gulf between testing an opinion and justifying a transaction price. The integrity of the valuation is lost in this gulf.

There is no evidence to suggest that this danger affects those with greater experience more than those less experienced colleagues. It can be argued both ways from first principles: it may well be that the danger is smaller for those who more readily rely on their own judgement, though it may be that in dispensing with much analysis they are more prone to the danger.

If experience is important, it needs to be understood what is the fruit, the content, of that experience. According to Adair and McGreal (1986: 42) valuers' experience 'over time produces an empathy for movements in the market, and allows the experienced valuer to reconcile differences among comparable sales evidence and so produce an accurate opinion of value.' In doing so, the valuer has to allow for the 'measure of inconsistency in any group of comparables, arising from variations in the subjective judgements of individual purchasers' (Swift, 1992: 88). This is no small task, and Millington (1994: 84) warns the valuer of placing too much faith in the comparable evidence at all, noting that '...past evidence might be of only very limited assistance or in extreme circumstances it might be positively misleading'.

Thus there is more to manage than data about the property revealed through inspection and the comparable evidence in formulating an opinion of value. Considerations about market dynamics, the prospects of the sub-region or region, unquantified aspects of the security itself and the perceptions of the valuer are all synthesised.

There is no doubt that valuers develop some sort of empathy for market movements but in this context the absence of the routine use of economic data within the appraisal process is significant. Mention has been made of the concentration in the comparables selection and analysis processes on the supply-side variables. Valuers spend much of their time producing a physical survey of the property and they collect far more data than is required merely for a valuation. This focus on the supply-side is decidedly at the expense of demand factors. This is in marked contrast to the US, where appraisal forms require data such as employment and wage trends and the prices of stocks and bonds.

The UK fascination with bricks and mortar is all the more surprising when one remembers the relatively fixed nature of the supply of houses. The supply of finance and changes in demand are far more important to house prices. Because they are not tracking these aggregates, valuers' 'empathy for market movements' tends to be reactive and not proactive.

Of course empathy in relatively stable conditions is one thing. Dislocations in markets and structural changes that precipitate changes in market equilibria cannot be quantified in advance (and are rarely even anticipated). At such times, the difficulties sketched heretofore pale into insignificance. DCC as an approach broke down completely in the face of the broad market collapse of 1988/9 (Gronow *et al* 1996). Grissom and Diaz (1991) describe similar breakdowns in the United States in the 1930s, in the 1970s and again in the 1980s. What characterised these earlier breakdowns was a movement by appraisers into alternative approaches of the type described in section 2.2 (typically variations on cost or investment-based approaches).

What uniquely characterised the UK experience of the late 1980s/early 1990s was precisely that no such alternatives were developed. Valuers clung to the DCC heuristic. They were able to do this precisely because, in reality, the DCC approach had been emasculated, reduced to validating the bid price. During the years of the markets' readjustment, validating the bidders' price – already the approach generally adopted – became the only option in the majority of cases.

Of course lenders did employ alternative strategies. For commercial property in such times, emphasis switches from the investment as security to the investor's covenant. Asimilar pressure occurred in residential lending in the 1990s and it is possible to envisage a continuing transfer of emphasis in risk management from the asset to the borrower.

2.7 DCC – a summary of pros and cons

DCC is almost invariably used in the appraisal of residential properties for mortgage purposes – in the UK it is practically the only method. It is clear that the method has certain strengths:

- In the form of an adjustment grid it is easily understood. Houses may be compared by reference to their attributes, housing transactions by reference to market conditions.
- It focuses the valuer on known quantities, earlier realised transaction prices and concurrent bids revealed in the market.
- Its application is not demanding where data is adequate. Valuers know how to use the method, the common processes are well documented and there is considerable scope for an artful interpretation of the method (see for example Dennett, 1997).

However, because of the nature of practice there has been (and there still is) a problem (see Chapter 3). DCC works best when there is copious data, yet even in the best of times such data is often sparse. At times when market equilibria are changing, the heuristic tends to break down completely. Not only does the supply of comparable data dry up, but also underlying assumptions about market stability are invalidated. In the absence of explicit treatment of demand-side data, the heuristic atrophies.

In its current form, DCC is analogous to the method of personnel recruitment that was used prior to the development of psychometric and other testing methods: the candidate with greatest presence was selected – normally the tallest man! In DCC the selection is normally the highest bid!

DCC enthusiasts should draw up an action programme to ensure that:

- the property data question is addressed;
- a more systematic and thorough use of available data is implemented; and
- the approach is developed to enable rational use in non-stable market conditions. This would lead, among other things, to much greater consideration of demand-side attributes and time series analysis.

DCC detractors might ask, with Adair and McGreal (1986: 43), if, in lieu of this, 'can an objective analysis of sales data assist the valuer in supporting the valuer in his opinion of market value?' This will entail some form of statistical analysis. Or, as were Grissom and Diaz (1991), they might be led to look to the development of cost-based and investment-based alternatives.

Given that housing costs are vitally important to all economic activity, all reasonable alternatives should be explored. The experience in the UK of the 'decade of negative equity' should have established this beyond dispute.

In Chapter 4 possible supplementary and alternative approaches are discussed that address some of the criticisms raised so far. In the next chapter, attention is turned to the market that supplies appraisal advice on the assumption that not only technical but also structural problems have contributed to past and ongoing difficulties. In the final section of this chapter, attention turns to the 'attributes' that impact on value.

2.8 Classification of attributes that impact on value

The valuer's mantra that value is dependent on location, location and location is a useful starting point for the development of a classification of attributes that impact on value.

It is clear that some factors that affect prices are determined at a national level. Aggregate measures of the wealth and performance of an economy and future expectations are likely to be important, as are government policies and the taxation and financial frameworks, particularly rules governing lending. *Ceteris paribus*, rates of interest have a direct and inverse bearing on capital values and they tend to apply nationally.

Given that identical properties in different regions vary considerably in price, it is clear that regional differences are important to price determination. Indeed, the regional median house price may be regarded as some measure of the wealth of the region. (International comparisons of house prices also reveal considerable national and regional variation but, given differences in culture, predisposition to buy or rent and different legal and financial frameworks, the use of raw house price data as a comparative measure of wealth is complicated.)

The factors that impact on house prices at this aggregate level are related to the following:

- the stock of houses and its net rate of increase or decrease;
- the population, its net rate of change, age distribution and economic activity;
- 'family' structure;
- the level of employment and rates of job formation and loss, and occupational structure;
- the level of domestic investment in non-housing investment instruments;
- measures of infrastructure 'wealth' and the rate of infrastructure development;
- expectations about economic growth;
- the redistributive effects of regional policy;
- perceptions of the supply of cultural stimulation;
- climate and topology;
- political stability etc.

The risk associated with region appears to be growing, because of the 'footloose-ness' of industry in a global market and because of the extent to which information and communication technologies enable commercial activity to be 'distributed'. A theoretical basis for modelling regional house prices would appear to be remote (Meen and Andrew, 1998).

Price variation for identical properties at the sub-regional level is also observable and stimulated the early work on trade-off between housing versus travel-to-work costs. Factors impacting on house prices at this level include

- accessibility to work and other foci for social intercourse;
- the level of provision of amenities and rates of local taxation;
- environmental quality;
- social values and aspirations, social cohesion, ethnicity, etc.

Risk associated with this aggregate will also grow as communication technologies begin to impact on the traditional structures of cities and towns, though given the high degree of inertia this will develop slowly.

Price variation is also observed at a fourth locational abstraction, that of neighbourhood. Important factors here are:

- access to nodes on transport networks;
- the quality of local schools and other facilities;
- levels of crime and perceptions of anti-social behaviour;
- security;
- landscape and layout;
- density of development;
- air quality;
- social class (different social strata exhibit strong tendencies to cluster).

A fifth locational layer, vicinity, where natural and/or man-made influences are important to price, is also identifiable. Among the factors which distinguish transactions are:

- poor ground conditions;
- mine shafts;
- soil erosion;
- preserved trees;
- lakes and conservation areas;
- electricity sub-stations;
- localised visual, noxious and noise pollutants;
- bad neighbours etc.

This class of attributes calls for a different approach in the appraisal process. Whether the variation is positive or negative, each may have a significant impact on value. These are some of the troublesome factors that cause 'distortion' in statistical studies and need to be identified by data models prior to inclusion or exclusion.

Overlaying the locational is a sectoral segmentation of markets. The factors that impact on the price of dwelling types are, analogous to location, related to the supply and demand functions within these segments. Different social groups express preferences for differing modes of dwelling and exhibit needs for different amounts and types of spaces, eg older people derive greater utility from bungalows and from sheltered and managed provision; environmental quality, aspect and tranquillity may command a premium.

Market research describing sectorally important attributes dependent on lifecycle stage, gender, social class, etc has proliferated in recent years. Such studies appear to uncover a blend of deeply felt and persistent requirements (eg spaciousness) as well as more transient needs (eg access to fibre optic cable networks).

Factors that relate to the property itself, the substance of most analysis, are many and various. Broad classes relate to the construction, accommodation, services and amenities of the property. Construction issues encompass construction method and materials, performance and structural obsolescence. Accommodation is concerned with the overall sizes of plot and habitable area and the functional division of spaces. Services and amenities are concerned not only with the supply of water and energy to and within the property but also with amenities ancillary to accommodation provided for the enjoyment of property. Valuers take much care in this latter area because much in the way of amenity which the purchaser buys is not of enduring value in terms of the security of the asset. Vendors' agents sell 'homes' and 'lifestyles'.

As well as property characteristics, valuers are concerned to identify transaction characteristics, which relate to the tenure of the property, qualifications to the definition of OMV, charges and encumbrances on occupation and use, etc, as well as contingent matters like planning and building regulations.

In approaching an alternative appraisal system, consideration would need to be given to these various attributes within their appropriate locational, sectoral and property-specific contexts. The first step would be the utilisation of digests of information relevant to each level of abstraction that will then need to be tracked over time.

The ultimate goal of an intelligent alternative would include the synthesis of key attributes in a unified model that was able to approach value in a dynamic market, combining temporal, sectoral, physical and spatial attributes. If location, location and location is a useful starting point, hopefully it is clear that the classification of 'layers' in a unified model will have little to do with geography!

Notes

1 One example of such valuations is provided in Chapter 5 dealing with the investment valuation of housing portfolios held by residential social landlords.
2 *Dawkins (VO) v Royal Leamington Spa Corporation & Warwickshire County Council* (1961) 8 RRC 241–5.4.5; 6.611.
3 *Gilmore (VO) v Baker-Carr (No 2)* (1963) 10 RRC 205–6.6.15.
4 Of course in some moments of the market cycle there may be only one bid. However, the lender is not concerned if that bid is objectively too low. That is an issue for the vendor.
5 In practice, alternative search criteria are used (explicitly and implicitly) and are likely to be more important as the paradigm shift in information and communication technology impacts on residential choice. From observation it is clear that for less common property types, the locational aspects of the search are relaxed or even ignored.
6 A single overriding factor is an attribute (or perhaps a cluster of attributes) that makes an overwhelming contribution to the value of a property.
7 In the absence of this revealed transaction price it is interesting to note that valuers nevertheless impute a starting figure thus con-firming the prevalence of the anchoring approach (Jenkins, 1992).

References and further reading

Adair, A.S. (1992) 'The determination of significant variables in the valuation of residential properties.' Unpublished PhD thesis, University of Reading.
Adair, A.S. and McGreal, W.S. (1986) 'The direct comparison method of valuation and statistical variability', *Journal of Valuation*, 5(1), 41–8.
Adair, A.S. and McGreal, W.S. (1987) 'The application of multiple regression analysis in property valuation', *Journal of Valuation*, 6, 57–67.
Adair, A.S. and McGreal, W.S. (1995) *Investigation of the Influence of Property and Socio-Economic Variables on Residential Values and the Formulation of*

Valuation Models Based on Regression Analysis. Technical Report, Real Estate Studies Unit, School of the Built Environment, University of Ulster.

Almond, N.I. (1999) 'Local knowledge in the valuation of residential property.' Unpublished PhD thesis, University of Glamorgan.

Almond, N.I. Jenkins, D.H. and Gronow, S.A. (1998) 'Development of a prototype residential valuation system', in *Computers in Urban Planning and Management*, Vol. 1. New Delhi and London: Narosa Publishing.

Antwi, A. (1995) 'Hedonic price indices', *Estates Gazette*, 9543, 124–6.

Appraisal Institute (1994) *Appraising Residential Properties*, 2nd edn. Chicago: Appraisal Institute.

Baum, A.E. and Crosby, N. (1995) *Property Investment Appraisal.* London: Routledge.

Baum, A.E. and Sams, G. (1997) *Statutory Valuations.* London: International Thomson Business Press.

Britton, W., Davies, K. and Johnson, T. (1989) *Modern Methods of Valuation of Land, Houses and Buildings*, 8th edn. London: Estates Gazette.

Czernkowski, R. (1990) 'Expert systems in real estate valuation', *Journal of Valuation*, 8(4), 376–93.

Darlow, C. (1988) *Valuation and Development Appraisal.* London: Estates Gazette.

Dennett, R.M. (1997) 'The development of a fully integrated information technology solution to the residential property valuation process.' Unpublished MPhil thesis, University of Glamorgan.

Eade, C. (1995) 'House price statistics contradict each other', *Property Week*, 28 September, p. 17.

Frampton, R. (1994) 'Valuation and the American way', *Estates Gazette*, 9402, 52–3.

Gallimore, P. (1994) 'Aspects of information processing in valuation judgement and choice', *Journal of Property Research*, 11, 97–110.

Greaves, M. (1984) 'The determinants of residential values: the hierarchical and statistical approaches', *Journal of Valuation*, 3, 5–23.

Grissom, T.V. and Diaz, J. (1991) *Real Estate Valuation: Guide to Investment Strategies.* New York: John Wiley.

Gronow, S.A., Ware, J.A., Jenkins, D.H., Lewis, O.M. and Almond, N.I. (1996) *A Comparative Study of Residential Valuation Techniques and the Development of a House Value Model and Estimation System.* Report for ESRC, Glamorgan.

Hendershott, P. (1994) *Valuing properties when comparable sales do not exist and the market is in disequilibrium.* The Cutting Edge Proceedings 1994, London: RICS.

James, C. (1997) *How Do You Do? An Introduction to Professional Knowledge and Its Development.* University of Glamorgan.

Jamieson, B. (1996) 'Lies, damn lies and house prices', *Sunday Telegraph*, 1 September, p. 17.

Jenkins, D.H. (1992) 'Expert systems in the land strategy of Cardiff City Council.' Unpublished MPhil thesis, Polytechnic of Wales.

Jenkins, D.H. and Gronow, S. (1990) 'Knowledge-based valuations', *Journal of Property Valuation and Investment*, 9(1), 90–9.

Jones Lang Wooton and South Bank Polytechnic (1989) *The Glossary of Property Terms*. London: Estates Gazette.

Kahneman, D., Slovic, P. and Tversky, A. (1982) *Judgement Under Uncertainty: Heuristics and Biases*. Cambridge: Cambridge University Press.

Knight, Frank (1996) *What Clinches a Deal*. Press release No. 66/96.

Mackmin, D. (1994) *The Valuation and Sale of Residential Property*, 2nd edn. London: Routledge.

Maclennan, D (1982) *Housing Economics*. London: Longman.

Meen, G. and Andrew, M. (1998) *Modelling Regional House Prices: A Review of the Literature*. London DETR.

Millington, A.F. (1994) *An Introduction to Property Valuation*, 4th edn. London: Estates Gazette.

Rees, W.H. (1992) *Valuation: Principles into Practice*, London: Estates Gazette.

Reynolds, A. (1984) 'Current valuation techniques', *The Valuer*, July, 198–204.

Richmond, D. (1994) *Introduction to Valuation*, 3rd edn. London: Macmillan.

Royal Institution of Chartered Surveyors (1995) *Appraisal and Valuation Manual*. London: RICS.

Schön, D.A. (1991) *The Reflective Practitioner*, 2nd edn. Aldershot: Arena.

Scott, I.P. (1988) 'A knowledge based approach to the computer-assisted mortgage valuation of residential property.' Unpublished PhD thesis, Polytechnic of Wales.

Shenkel, W.M. (1978) *Modern Real Estate Appraisal*. New York and London: McGraw-Hill.

Slovic, P. and Lichtenstein, S. (1971) 'Comparison of Bayesian and regression approaches to the study of the information processing in judgement', *Organisational Behaviour and Human Performance*, 6, 649–744.

Stillings, N.A., Feinstein, M.H., Garfield, J.L., Rissland, E.L., Rosenbaum, D.A., Weisler, S.E. and Baker-Ward, L. (1995) *Cognitive Science: An Introduction*, 2nd edn. Cambridge, MA and London: MIT Press.

Swift, N. (1992) 'Beyond approximation', *Estates Gazette*, 9241, 88–90.

Tversky, A. and Kahneman, D. (1974) 'Judgement under uncertainty: heuristics and biases', *Science*, 185, 1124–31.

Waxman, P. and Lenard, D. (1994) *Investing in Residential Property: Understanding the Market in the 1990s*, 3rd edn. Elsternwick: Wrightbooks.

Wolverton, M. and Diaz, J. (1996) *Investigation into Price Knowledge Induced Comparable Selection Bias*, Cutting Edge Conference. London:RICS.

Chapter 3

The Supply of Valuation Advice

3.1 Overview

This chapter is concerned with the supply of valuation advice.
Sections 3.2 and 3.3 are concerned with the relationship between
the supply of advice and the development of valuation method and
practice in recent times. The contention here is that changes in the
supply side for valuation advice have contributed directly to the
diluted valuation method that was described in the last chapter.
Key developments in the supply side are reviewed and the impacts
of the changes on valuation method are assessed.

Sections 3.4 and 3.5 respectively attempt to reappraise the
objective interests of lenders and consumers in a contemporary
context, while section 3.6 offers some remedial suggestions that may
be helpful in securing the place of independent, objective appraisals
in the housing market. Section 3.7 then looks forward to changes in
the supply of advice that flow from government proposals and the
development of e-commerce.

3.2 Supplying valuation advice

The current shape of mortgage valuation services in the UK owes
much to the development of financial institutions, not a little to the
courts that have developed modern contract and tort law and some
to the professional bodies that represent the interests of surveyors.[1]

The original context of a mortgage valuation was the legal
requirement of building societies, under section 13 of the Building
Societies Act 1986, to be in receipt of a written valuation. Typically a
mortgage valuation is conducted by a valuer employed by a lender
or by a panel valuer under contract to a lender. Seldom will the purchaser of property commission a valuation survey independently.

There is no space here for a review of historical developments.
Interested readers are referred to MMC (1994) and Byrom (1979) for
a fuller history. However, it is necessary to review the most recent,
significant developments in order to understand current practice.
These developments were as follows.

3.2.1 The deregulation of the financial services industry in the UK during the 1980s

This has had three profound effects.

First, in place of a paternalistic oligopoly deregulation promoted competition in the supply of mortgage funds. According to the Monopolies and Mergers Commission (MMC, 1994) there were more than 150 residential mortgage lenders in the UK in 1994 in a highly competitive market. Logically an increase in the supply of funds was likely, *ceteris paribus*, to give rise to asset price inflation in the short term, while more competition in such circumstances might induce a relaxation of risk controls. Arguably both these effects have occurred.

The second effect was more relevant to the concerns of this chapter. It changed the pattern of the supply of advice. Traditionally small firms of locally based chartered surveyors/ incorporated valuers conducted mortgage valuations. Very often these firms also had an agency role and were thus very familiar with the local markets in which they operated. This pattern was disrupted by two separate developments. Lenders acquired estate agencies as a front line for the capture of mortgage business and other services – this had the effect of severing agency and mortgage valuation. At the same time the lenders began to grow their own in-house valuation teams as well as to tighten control over the use of independent 'panel' valuers.

During the market downturn of the early 1990s the panel valuers began to see business reduce as in-house valuation teams and valuation subsidiaries of the lenders took a larger share. Some RICS members' concerns of a conflict of interest were founded on the observation that the lender as agent was setting asking prices and as mortgage valuer was verifying bid prices.

The MMC concluded that this potential conflict of interest had not materialised. Controls within lending organisations had been designed to prevent this conflict and were ruled to be effective (despite the views of many smaller firms of chartered surveyors). However, if true, this led to a further severance of the agency and valuation roles. Valuation staffs were left without the key information required for prudent appraisal.

The third effect was that many building societies converted to banks and therefore broke free of the Building Society Act that had historically shaped valuation business. The lenders and their valuation subsidiaries were given considerable scope for reshaping the supply of valuation advice, though movement has been slow. Both in-house teams and subsidiaries have been relatively profitable and in the absence of consumer concern, inertia has been the dominant force.

3.2.2 The development of mortgage indemnity insurance

The top slice of a secured loan is exposed to greater risk. Traditionally the forced sale of assets by lenders following borrower default results in losses that can become severe in a recessionary phase of the cycle. This insurance product removes much of the risk from lenders at the expense of those borrowers requiring higher loan to asset value ratios (typically loans in excess of 75% of market value).

3.2.3 The concern of the courts to ensure that the consumer, the house-buyer, has some form of redress in cases where valuers have been negligent in the exercise of their duty

The judgement in *Smith* v *Eric S Bush*; *Harris* v *Wyre Forest District Council* [1990] 1 AC 831 established beyond doubt that a surveyor engaged by a building society to carry out a mortgage valuation owes a duty of care to a purchaser as well as to the lender. (The argument articulated by the courts is that the surveyor knows that the purchaser will rely on this valuation regardless of whether the purchaser receives a copy of the report.)

However, the valuer's primary duty is to the lender who has commissioned the report. Following the collapse of the housing market in the late 1980s, the extent of that liability has been a major issue for valuers while lenders have been reviewing their stance in relation to the provision of valuation services in order to minimise their exposure to claims of negligence. Contrary to the advice of the MMC (1994: 153), lenders now routinely withhold valuation reports and no longer charge the borrower a valuation fee directly. (It has been 'absorbed' into the interest rate.)

Other court judgements had a direct but unanticipated impact on the way in which valuers conducted their business. Most actions against valuers in the 1980s were concerned not with the exercise of their skill in appraisal but survey.

In a string of decisions (eg *Roberts* v *J Hampson & Co* [1989] 2 All ER 510) the courts made it clear that surveyors were liable for failure to disclose defects to premises. Given that the price of surveys was unchanged, that no additional surveying resource was injected into the process and that there was no measurable increase in productivity, the balance of the surveyor's effort in producing a report swung toward inspection leaving less resource for appraisal.

Decisions regarding appraisal tended to reinforce that effect. It had long been recognised by the courts that 'valuation is an art, not a science' and that there is a 'permissible margin of error, the "bracket"'.[2] Subsequent decisions concerned the size of the bracket: a valuation within 15% either side of the market price was deemed reasonable. In the residential context this gave considerable comfort to valuers and one may postulate that concern for accuracy in respect of valuation was further undermined.

3.2.4 *The traditional role of the RICS/ ISVA of safeguarding professional standards was partly usurped by the lenders themselves*

The very high level of claims against valuers (Mason and Rice, 1996) prompted the professional bodies to review practice but this was insufficient for the lenders. The panel system became more rigorous in the selection of professional firms (MMC, 1994). A further development was the establishment of busy 'Claims Sections' by lenders to deal with purchasers' losses arising from mistakes in survey reports by in-house and panel valuers.

3.3 Impact on valuation practice and method

The emphasis on survey rather than appraisal conditioned by the decisions of the courts came at a time of increased competition between lenders. Report turnaround time might be critical to winning business. Lenders expected valuers to work more quickly and turn over more cases per day.

At the same time lenders were conducting an increasing proportion of mortgage appraisal business directly or through their subsidiaries. The link between agency and valuation was severed and with it the local or sectoral market intelligence that valuers traditionally applied in the decision-making process. In fact some valuers began to be employed over such wide geographic areas that the RICS was forced to introduce a 'local knowledge' component into the definition of competence for practice.

The natural tendency for UK surveyors to focus on the supply side – the bricks and mortar – was further exaggerated at precisely the moment that precious demand-side knowledge was atrophying. In such circumstances it is clear to see why, if corners were to be cut, the appraisal not the survey process would be the prime candidate. The outcomes are described in Chapter 2: the formal analysis of comparables did not happen, bid prices were revealed to valuers, and the vast majority of valuations endorse bid prices or amend them marginally with one eye fixed presumably on the 'bracket' for permissible error.

The severance of the relationship between agency and valuation would have had less impact if transaction data had been more widely available. An essential tool for the valuer in using DCC is the availability of a database of comparable sales. The lack of public availability of transaction data from the Land Registry in England and Wales and the objective need for professional access to reliable data are issues that have been argued consistently by academics and are starting to be addressed.

Critical to an appreciation of current weaknesses in residential appraisal is that a healthy information regime (local valuers with access to local agency data) has disappeared and has not yet been replaced. Delivering objective valuations from limited data always required considerable skill. Having undermined that skill-base the next best solution would be a substitute method that was able to utilise small amounts of data,[3] and failing that a substitute method that was able to use extensive data. These topics are the focus of the next chapter.

3.4 The lender's interest in a valuation and survey

Lenders have one objective interest in the valuation and survey of real estate: the value of an asset as security. Clearly lenders are concerned about the value at the date of a loan, but they are also concerned about the future value of the asset, its sustainable value. For this reason lenders are not entirely satisfied with the use of open market value (OMV) as the measure of mortgage value. At the very least they would like to see opinions 'about factors which might affect the value of a property several years into the life of a loan' (Billingham, 1997). Objectively they require a different measure of value, a longer-run equilibrium value.

Of course, lenders are not so concerned about the value toward

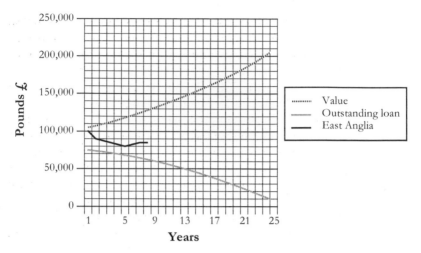

Figure 3.1 Capital repayments mapped against value growth. The shorter solid line is based on DoE mix-adjusted house prices by region and applies average percentage changes for East Anglia between 1989 and 1996 to an asset valued at £100,000

the end of the amortisation period. The longer that any loan lasts, *ceteris paribus*, the less exposed is the lender to a risk of loss on default. Historically, house prices in western economies have risen over the long run. Assuming annual growth in house prices of only 3% (well below the trend figure and close to UK government inflation targets) a residence exchanging hands at £100,000 today will be worth over £200,000 at the end of a typical 25-year mortgage. In fact over the last 25 years the average UK house price has risen by a factor of 10 from £7,300 in 1972 to £75,600 in 1997 (Source: DoE mix-adjusted house prices).

The graph in Figure 3.1 shows capital repayments (longer solid line) mapped against value growth for the asset described above (dotted line) where the repayment rate of interest is 7% and the growth rate is 3%. In the case of a 75% loan (and this is the maximum exposure of the lender since mortgage indemnity insurance became the norm) perhaps the comfort zone for a lender is reached during year 4. The shorter solid line shows the worst case scenario for short-term regional average house price depreciation in the UK in the twentieth century (falls in nominal house prices occurred for the only time in the UK between 1989 and 1995: they were sharpest in East Anglia, the source for this data).

The clear implication is that lenders entertain low risk in relation to the value of housing assets and that the current procedure of survey and valuation is conducted because it is profitable rather than objectively necessary.

A number of provisos must be expressed about Figure 3.1. The shorter, solid line (East Anglia) applies percentage changes to an asset valued at £100,000, though the percentage changes relate to a measure of central tendency (the average value of a house in East Anglia in 1989 was £75,300). Of course every measure of central tendency implies that many cases fall below the measure, so that many houses in East Anglia will have depreciated in value by greater percentages, so great perhaps that the lender may have experienced negative equity and, in the case of default, loss. Nevertheless, on past evidence it is clear that the mortgage valuation survey became a hammer to crack a nut.

This is not to suggest that lenders are uninterested in value (though for commercial purposes it is the portfolio and not the individual transaction that matters). Nor is it the case that future policy in this area should be determined in relation to past evidence alone. However, the task of lenders and their advisers is to pinpoint the source of the risk and measure it.

Most property risk comes from economic obsolescence, defined as a loss in real value due to economic and social changes (we are not concerned here with borrower risk, credit rating, etc). A number of factors suggest that house price variations may be less predictable in the future. In the global economy, job security and income are far less stable: regional and sub-regional price changes may be sudden and dramatic. In the UK housing market there are more properties than households, while the rate of annual household formation is currently slowing and will slow more substantially over the next decade (Ermisch, 1991). At the same time there is a mismatch between demand and supply in geographic terms. There are changing patterns of migration. Regional policies and priorities are under review. All these structural and sectoral price changes add uncertainty to prediction.

Such risks are best assessed through house price forecasts based on explicit supply- and demand-side data at regional and urban aggregates. Such exercises do not require individual property inspections (though, arguably, a belt and braces approach might involve a loss on forced sale valuation.)

Some property risk stems from physical obsolescence and this type of risk is identified only through survey. However, physical obsolescence is rarely an issue in financial terms over the life of a mortgage. From the perspective of the lender it is necessary to ensure that the borrower does not neglect or wilfully damage property. The lender's interest can be safeguarded in this respect through the mortgage contract or by an insurance policy.

3.5 The borrower's interest in a valuation and survey

Unlike lenders, borrowers have a variety of objective interests in the valuation and survey of property. Like lenders they are concerned about the longer-term value of a house. Traditionally, this involves an expectation of capital appreciation. However, borrowers may be willing to entertain stable or falling values, depending on other objectives.

Objectively, buyers are also concerned about value for money, structural adequacy, repair costs, costs in use and the suitability of a property for their requirements. Yet most consumers receive direct advice on practically none of these things. There is a gap between their needs and the satisfaction of them. This is probably because transaction costs are already so high that most consumers rely on lenders to assess risk.

Objectively, however, the borrower's risk is far greater than the lender's – there is no 25% cushion supplied by mortgage indemnity insurance. If a borrower took out a 100% loan on our £100,000 property and did not default, then on the East Anglia example in Figure 3.1, (s)he would have enjoyed real negative equity in each of the first eight years of the loan (at least) peaking at £15,000 in year 5 (a 90% loan would have generated zero or negative equity for six years peaking at £5,700 in year 5). Should the borrower default, (s)he remains liable for payment of any shortfall (CML, 1998). What many borrowers paying premia did not realise was that not only did the benefit of mortgage indemnity insurance accrue to the lender, but also that the insurance companies could and would pursue borrowers for the full amount they had paid out to lenders claiming under such policies.

The suggestion is that the borrower needs to exercise greater caution. And value is not the only issue. Any expense incurred in maintaining or remedying the structure, fabric or finishings of the building will fall to the consumer (unless they were overlooked by a surveyor acting negligently or have been insured against). Objectively the consumer needs a thorough valuation and survey.

3.6 Remedial suggestions

The current mismatch between objective interests and market practice may be corrected by market mechanisms in the fullness of time as consumers become aware of the degree of their exposure and as lenders, under the pressure of reducing margins, refine their risk calculations. Nevertheless the erosion of the historic coincidence of interest between lenders and borrowers suggests that the market might be lightly regulated to ensure that consumers receive independent advice.

In any event the RICS could take action regarding the dilution of method in the appraisal stage of the valuation. A code of practice to ensure that acceptable methods are being followed is overdue.

Consideration could also be given to a local licensing system to ensure that practitioners are competent to perform in a geographic area. This licensing should be independent of vested interests. (Similar, though not identical, forms of regulation occur in the United States.)

A national database of all house transactions should be independently maintained and accessible to licensed practitioners.

The measure of value – OMV – should be reviewed. Spot prices are hardly suitable for measuring sustainable value.

Given earlier comments about the lack of a coherent professional and academic approach to the discipline of residential appraisal, it may be sensible to establish a well-defined degree course, accredited by professional bodies and regulated by a dedicated division of the RICS, despite the opposition of some members of the RICS. Such a course would need to take cognisance of the changes underway in the house buying and selling process described in the next section. In terms of business process re-engineering, it may now be more efficient to professionalise estate agency, thus reforging the link between agency and valuation, and acknowledge that the existing two-stage process is under pressure.

3.7 The changing nature of the marketplace for valuation advice

Government concerns to speed the process of house purchase and to reduce costs to consumers are likely to further impact on the supply of valuation advice.

In the short term many valuation practices are licking their lips at the prospect of a seller's pack that contains, *inter alia*, survey data on properties. It would certainly appear that in the short term valuers expect to be invited to perform initial surveys for vendors and subsequent valuation surveys for lenders. For how long the market will tolerate this additional burden is not clear.

It is not unimaginable that lenders seeking a competitive edge would wish to rely at law on the survey produced for vendors in the appraisal process. Lenders' current degree of control over surveying quality would be swapped for a legally enforceable claim against independent surveyors backed by professional indemnity insurance. In such a scenario, lenders would revise their appraisal procedures so that their focus is once again trained more specifically on transaction risk (hopefully expressed in a measure of sustainable value).

In this scenario buyers receive no independent advice regarding value, the status quo ante, unless they are prepared to pay for it. Surveyors would need to sharpen marketing techniques in order to sell services to buyers (also reflecting the status quo).

Of course these outcomes are far from certain. The lenders' strategy may be totally other. In a second scenario, the lenders might decide to offer surveys to vendors with guaranteed advances to the 'right' purchasers. In this scenario there would be a 'collision' of estate agents and lenders, and purchasers would clearly need independent advice.

The government's proposals are still tentative. What is more certain is that e-commerce will play a major role in shaping the market for the supply of advice. The growth of the Internet is phenomenal. And the rate of growth will be greater as access to cyber-markets increases. The advent of new modes of access (TV, games consoles, intelliphones) will ensure that an increasing number of consumers has direct access to markets. At the same time new intermediaries will develop to provide services for the 'information excluded' and added value for consumers requiring more sophisticated products.

There is considerable concurrent activity, sufficient to give an indication of the shape of things to come in the short term. The first impact of e-commerce is to revolutionise supply chains.

Market intermediaries deal primarily in information. The best market-makers offer competitively priced, reliable information in ways that are readily appreciated and easily accessed by consumers. Before the year 2000 new forms of intermediary (like the eMortgage Network) and new alliances emerged (eg Nationwide and HM Land Registry's steps towards electronic conveyancing). Initially service providers will improve existing services.

For example, house sellers typically visit or call a selection of estate agents. Informed sellers are interested in the agent's fee, perceptions of market-making ability and the likely price of the asset. Estate agents, key players in markets for appraisal advice, are based in high streets close to masses of consumers. Their windows are filled with pictures of the product with indicative price data. Consumers wishing to buy, generally speaking, visit a selection of such agents, acquire a selection of property details and then visit a selection of those properties. This research is a time consuming and costly process.

Already, vendors, agents and buyers are trying alternative routes. Vendors are able to advertise homes directly on a website. They may provide their own property description, photographs and bid price or they may ask an agent's advice (sometimes without payment!). Agents, alive to the new 'threat', are creating their own websites or posting their property details on a host website (like CountyWeb in the UK). Consumers are able to search the Internet and select properties by location, price/rent and tenure preference, and in time they will be able to use other search criteria that better reflect their aspirations.

Of course, the move to e-commercial media may not be as swift as the analagous move to Internet booksellers, like Amazon.com. The nature of the product is an important element. Books are small and relatively inexpensive. Not much advice is required in purchasing decisions. Houses are important investments and substantial assets so that investment and survey advice is necessary. Houses are also homes that need to be viewed and experienced. One might buy a book without touching it, less likely so a house. Successful e-commercial home sellers will therefore need to offer, directly or indirectly, reliable surveying and financial services and products or advice about them. They will also need to ensure that search costs are reduced for consumers and that the purchasing experience is enhanced.

This points the way to the development of new e-commercial products within estate agency. The early moves can be seen simply as a scramble to establish some auxiliary Internet-based add-on to traditional business. A maturing market will see the development of web-based geographic information systems (GIS) that allow consumers to acquire considerable knowledge of locational attributes. Visualisation software will permit consumers to look around a neighbourhood and inside a property remotely. Appraisal software will inform purchasers of values, trends and finance deals – and all before leaving the Internet access point and visiting a single house.

It is by no means clear who will supply these services. Possible candidates include lenders, estate agents, other financial or legal intermediaries and software houses/Internet value-added resellers. The shape of the market for the supply of that advice is all to play for.

Such developments will not necessarily be driven by accretions of software. One of the key features of the Internet has been its capacity to enable the forging of global alliances of people with common interests. Social change inevitably follows changes in technology and communication. There is therefore the possibility, for example, of new forms of common ownership in financial assets. At a time when mutuality in mortgage lending is atrophying in the UK market, it is possible that the Internet will enable a new mutual movement.

Whatever the shape of the market, objectively vendors, purchasers and lenders will require appraisal information. The role of government is to ensure that such markets are adequately regulated so that objective interests are met without monopoly effects and that consumers receive appropriate, independent professional advice.

Notes

1   While the professional bodies also represent the interests of consumers vicariously by regulating surveying practice, they are unable to do this consistently because of other vested interests.
2   Watkins J in *Singer & Friedlander* v *John D. Wood & Co* (1977) 243 EG 212.
3. Linear programming (Wiltshaw, 1991), MRA (multiple regression analysis) and neural networks have been suggested but have not been accepted within the profession.

References

Billingham, E. (1997) 'Bankers call for radical changes to Red Book', *Estates Gazette*, 9708, 53.

Byrom, R.J. (1979) *The Building Society Valuer: Including the Survey and Valuation of Houses and Flats for Owner Occupation*. London: Estates Gazette.

CML(1998) 'Mortgage indemnity: a borrower's guide', www.cml.org.uk/faqs/mig.htm.

Ermisch, J. (1991) 'An ageing population, household formation and housing', *Housing Studies*, 6, 230–40.

Mason, J. and Rice, R. (1996) 'Property valuers win landmark ruling', *Financial Times*, 21 June, p. 8.

Monopolies and Mergers Commission (1994) *The Supply of Residential Mortgage Valuations*. London: HMSO.

Wiltshaw, D.G. (1991) 'Valuation by comparable sales and linear algebra', *Journal of Property Research*, 8, 3–19.

Chapter 4

The Development of Valuation Technique

4.1 Overview

In Chapter 2 it was suggested that the valuer's task is to develop some measure of preference/value that expresses social or market requirements of housing. Most of Chapter 2 was devoted to a critique of the existing method of calculating open market value, namely DCC. What characterises this method is the selection of small amounts of focused data that are used to justify opinion. Section 4.2 describes software for DCC that addresses some of the problems identified in the critique.

However, an alternative strategy would be to analyse large amounts of more broadly based data and then measure the current transaction in terms of the whole. This may be an especially relevant strategy where the concern is to identify sustainability of the particular (value) in the light of the whole.[1] Such a strategy is typical of mass appraisal where the objective is to produce values for complete sub-markets (eg for taxation purposes). It follows that a review of mass appraisal techniques may be useful in developing a method for mortgage valuations.

Consequently section 4.3 provides a brief review of mass appraisal techniques applied to residential appraisal. Section 4.4 outlines a strategy that is aimed at developing an intelligent alternative to DCC. Sections 4.5–4.8 report on progress to date in developing the strategy (in lay terms), aspects of which are presented in greater detail (and more technical language) in the Appendix. Section 4.9 provides a conclusion to this chapter.

4.2 DCC by 'expert' database

Computerised database tools are well established in the business community. They deserve mention here because their full potential for the appraisal community is yet to be realised. According to an RICS study, over 80% of GP surveyors use a PC in connection with their work, mostly for word processing and database packages (around 60% use one regularly) (Honey, 1997). A Glamorgan survey conducted in 1998 shows that in the residential sector, 44% of administration systems are now computerised though databases designed specifically for appraisal purposes are lagging behind at 30% of respondents.

There is also scope for greatly intensified use. Most surveyors use their PCs for two hours or less per day, only 9% use computers in the field, and less then 7% use any form of statistical analysis on their data.

Additionally, because database techniques are at the heart of the comparative process, they offer an intuitive, anthropomorphic solution to some of the problems associated with DCC. Theoretically there must be opportunities for database technologies within a valuation profession that stands by DCC.

Indeed, there is a growing use of databases for storing and searching comparables data. However, simply modelling the deficient practice of DCC described above in a modern database will hardly address the problem. The opportunity needs to be taken to deal with as many known deficiencies of DCC as possible.

In order to explore the limits of DCC, the Glamorgan team developed a fully functional prototype database nicknamed Nimrod. The system is described more fully in Almond *et al* (1998).

Essentially data capture occurs on site using a palm-top PC with Windows CE™ operating system. This data is then fed to a desktop system for analysis and valuation. The analysis phase is triggered when the valuer performs a search for comparables. The search process can be launched 'manually' by user selection of appropriate search criteria, so that data may be retrieved by price range, location, tenure, building type, etc, simply or in combination. This is typical of the database technology that is found in existing practices. Alternatively the user can select an 'intelligent' search process. This launches a recursive trawl through data that identifies the closest matches on multiple attributes. In this approach the system has been programmed with rules elicited from valuers. It follows the search strategies that valuers would use if they followed their logic through to its time-consuming conclusion. These search strategies are not only efficient in the sense that they search on attribute hierarchies that the valuers define, but also are sensitive in that they are able to map value structures across regions that valuers are able to articulate. The tendency to anchor on specific transactions is circumvented as the search strategy identifies the most useful comparables. Figure 4.1 shows selected comparables and their attributes in comparison with a subject property.

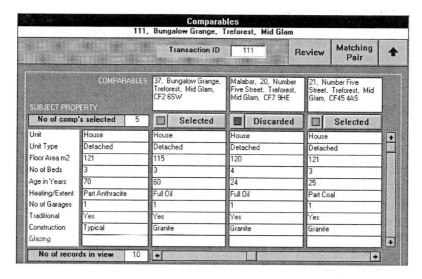

	COMPARABLES	37, Bungalow Grange, Treforest, Mid Glam, CF2 6SW	Malabar, 20, Number Five Street, Treforest, Mid Glam, CF7 9HE	21, Number Five Street, Treforest, Mid Glam, CF45 4AS
SUBJECT PROPERTY				
No of comp's selected	5	☐ Selected	■ Discarded	☐ Selected
Unit	House	House	House	House
Unit Type	Detached	Detached	Detached	Detached
Floor Area m2	121	115	120	121
No of Beds	3	3	4	3
Age in Years	70	60	24	25
Heating/Extent	Part Anthracite	Full Oil	Full Oil	Part Coal
No of Garages	1	1	1	1
Traditional	Yes	Yes	Yes	Yes
Construction	Typical	Granite	Granite	Granite
Glazing				
No of records in view	10			

Comparables
111, Bungalow Grange, Treforest, Mid Glam
Transaction ID 111   Review   Matching Pair

Figure 4.1 Comparables selected through automatic matching process

Having ranked transaction evidence in order of comparability, the software then presents the user with the type of adjustment grid described in Chapter 2 and illustrated in Figure 4.2. All attributes are displayed on screen and each can be adjusted manually (though theoretically the system could prompt adjustment where on-line cost or value data were available).

The system automatically looks up the transaction date of each comparable and adjusts the figure for time elapsed by reference to house price indices. Clearly this facility could be far more sophisticated to accommodate local market movements.

More useful perhaps is the availability on screen of data indicating market conditions at the time of each transaction (average time for a property to sell, interest rates, unemployment rates, etc). Linking such databases to exogenous sources of data will be one means by which value is added to the services supplied by professionals in the future. Ready access to such demand-side data also addresses a fundamental problem associated with traditional practice.

Geographic information systems (GIS) are a particular form of database that links transaction data to map background data. These systems allow valuers to visualise a geographic region and identify the spatial location of specific transactions. Valuers can overlay the boundaries of markets on maps. Search strategies can also be

		Analysis					
		111, Bungalow Grange, Treforest, Mid Glam					

| | | Transaction ID | 111 | | | Synopsis | |

SUBJECT PROPERTY	COMPARABLES	15, Bungalow Grange, Treforest, CF2 6SW		21, Number Five Street, Treforest, CF45 4AS		Hensol, 27, Bungalow Grange, Treforest, CF37 1EX	
Unit	House	House	0	House	0	House	0
Unit Type	Detached	Detached	0	Detached	0	Detached	0
Floor Area m2	121	115	500	121	0	127	-500
No of Beds	3	3	0	3	0	3	0
Age in Years	70	60	0	25	0	21	-350
Heating/Extent	Part Anthracite	Full Oil	-500	Part Coal	0	Part Coal	0
No of Garages	1	1	0	1	0	1	0
Traditional	Yes	Yes	0	Yes	0	Yes	0
Construction	Typical	Granite	0	Granite	0	Granite	0
Glazing							
Adjusted comparables values >		£70,091		£69,522		£69,356	
No of comp's selected	5						

Figure 4.2 Comparables adjustment

performed on maps. For example, drawing a shape on a map can be linked to a report on all the transactions available within the map area identified. These searches can be quite sophisticated. It is possible to link a polygon overlaying the map with attribute data so as, for example, to identify all the four-bed properties sold in the last six months within the area defined.

Nor is GIS an immature technology. The author first developed a GIS for residential valuation in 1988 (see Jenkins, Gronow and Prescott, 1989). The main advantages were that:

- the subject property and its comparables were easy to locate and relate;
- sub-markets could be readily identified and delineated;
- where topography, geology or development had a high impact on value, these factors were easy to identify or plot;
- more complex representations of the data were reasonably easy to develop, eg it is possible to generate value 'contours'; and
- to aid comparable selection it is possible to develop ripple algorithms that radiate out from the target property to the closest comparables in time, sector and space.

Databases are one of the tools that will assist in realising the RICS information strategy goal 'to promote a simpler, more transparent, property market and to improve decision-making'. But databases are only a building block for more sophisticated techniques that will allow professionals to maintain an edge and add value.

4.3 Mass appraisal to the rescue?

Multiple regression analysis (MRA) is one approach that has been used consistently in the valuation of residential properties for taxation purposes (see for example IAAO, 1978), though not for individual market valuations. The method requires the identification of a homogeneous area or market segment that affords a minimum of a hundred transactions; the dependent variable, price, is mapped against a limited number of key independent variables that are known to contribute to the value of properties in the area/segment. Software such as SPSS (Statistical Package for the Social Sciences) is able to derive a function that may then be used to value new properties where the key variables are known.

Techniques required to perform valuation using MRA can be assimilated in quite short timescales and many appraisal professionals in America, Australia and elsewhere use the approach routinely. The method is less prevalent in the UK. Of course, the analysis and valuation phases require that considerable care be taken in the selection of evidence and the preparation of data, though no more care perhaps than is required in the traditional DCC approach properly conducted.

More recently, artificial neural network (ANN) software has offered a similar strategy with similar results, though as few as 30 transactions may be sufficient to generate a useful function (James, 1994). Essentially ANNs identify patterns in data. The network is trained to identify the pattern, which is then represented by a function. The function is applied to a new case. As with MRA, software training needs to be coupled with an appreciation of data preparation issues.

Neural networks have been mooted as an alternative means of computing value for most of the 1990s. There have, however, been fundamental difficulties for their adoption, difficulties shared in some measure with MRA:

- They are not understood. No one teaches valuers why and how they are used.
- They require more data to calibrate than the selection of two or three comparables associated with DCC.

- When calibrated, they have been useful only for valuing properties in the same small patch as the original sample. The impression given therefore is that the additional effort yields little product.
- The internal workings of the network and the output are not as easily explained as in the traditional approach.
- There is a degree of arbitrariness. Different ANNs have been observed to yield quite different results. Also the same neural network has been observed to yield different quality outputs when applied to different data sets.

However, there are some distinct advantages:

- The networks are able to make use of demand and supply side data explicitly.
- The systems work speedily.
- The systems supply their own estimates of confidence.
- They have the *potential* to meet accuracy criteria.

Note that the stress here is on the *potential*. There is a margin of difference between a mass appraisal technique that provides reasonably fair estimates of value for all the properties in a population against a valuation technique for an individual property providing a measure of accuracy sufficient to satisfy a borrower.

4.4 A strategy to develop an intelligent valuation method

Early MRAand neural network studies used data from a single area or market because functions can become very elaborate when data is taken from a wide area, like a whole city. Even so, past studies have reported a high level of success. Average absolute error levels for neural network studies are commonly reported between 5 and 7.5%.

To meet the drawbacks, researchers at Glamorgan identified a series of objectives that need to be met if an alternative or supplementary approach is to be developed to DCC that is at once practicable and intelligible. Briefly stated, these objectives were:

- to break free from the limitations imposed by the study of a homogeneous area and obtain the maximum return from data (section 4.5);
- to represent within the functions developed some surrogates for demand and thereby move on from a debilitating reliance on past transaction/survey data alone (section 4.5);

- to build intelligibility into the process so that valuers feel comfortable using it and are aware of limitations (section 4.6);
- to harness more professional knowledge in order to provide an intelligent and human-friendly environment (section 4.6);
- to address cycles in property markets so that the system is conscious of trends and begins to offer forecasts (section 4.7);
- to circumvent the arbitrariness associated with the choice and operation of neural network platforms and system settings (section 4.8).

Considerably more work is required before such an alternative becomes a reality. Nevertheless progress has been made and the work reported in the remainder of the chapter and in the Appendix, conducted by the Glamorgan team, is offered as a contribution.

4.5 Modelling a heterogeneous market

To assume that there is a single, smooth and continuous valuation function underpinning the complex interaction of demand- and supply-side variables in a heterogeneous market would be an over-simplification. Instead, mass appraisal researchers assume that homogeneous sub-markets will contain less variance than the heterogeneous market and thus be more susceptible to accurate modelling.

A heterogeneous property market clearly contains a range of different housing types across strata of varied cultures, economies and environments. Valuation literature presents a number of arguments supporting the existence of identifiable sub-markets within a heterogeneous residential property market. The basic argument, in the words of Strazheim (1973), is: 'The urban housing market is, in fact, a set of compartmentalised and unique sub-markets'. The task is to identify or stratify them.

This requires stratification criteria (section 4.5.1) and strategies (section 4.5.2). Owen Lewis and Andrew Ware of the Glamorgan team undertook research into both before setting out an agenda for empirical work (section 4.5.3).

4.5.1 Stratification criteria

Stratification by location

The aim of stratification, in this case, is to segment the heterogeneous property market into homogeneous sub-markets with respect to locational and environmental aspects. This approach has been taken by a number of researchers (for example, Sauter, 1985; Adair and McGreal, 1987 and 1996; Eckert, 1990) and in the main, the results have shown that the sub-markets are more susceptible to accurate modelling than the overall market. However, care must be taken in ensuring that boundaries are carefully selected and a significant sample size is maintained (Eckert, 1990).

Stratification by property type

Here, the property market is partitioned with respect to property characteristics. Properties are grouped according to size, age, type, number of storeys (Adair and McGreal, 1995), number of rooms, state of repair, number of bathrooms, garage (Have *et al*, 1997).

Stratification by buyer behaviour

In the third case, described by Adair, Berry and McGreal (1996) as the 'behavioural' approach, segmentation is performed in respect of purchasers that are grouped according to 'identifiably different approaches to and valuations of various attributes' (Adair and McGreal, 1987).

4.5.2 Stratification strategies

Mass appraisal researchers employ a number of strategies to identify homogeneous markets, of which the following are found in published literature.

Manual selection of homogeneous areas

In this approach, data is carefully selected from a well-defined area believed to be homogeneous (homogeneity in this case is usually defined with respect to location and, therefore, encompasses environmental and econometric influences). This approach has been used to assess the usefulness of MRA, ANNs, linear programming and expert systems (Adair and McGreal, 1987; Evans *et al*, 1992; Wiltshaw, 1991; Gronow and Scott, 1985). Varying degrees of success have been achieved, and contributions to knowledge made with respect to the coding and representation of data (Borst, 1991; Gronow and Scott, 1985), the selection and transformation of influential variables (Adair and McGreal, 1987; Greaves, 1984), and generally introducing data analysis tools to the valuation community.

Unfortunately, manual stratification is limited by the inherent complexity of the market. To properly construct a homogeneous space requires a complete understanding of the interrelationships between the demand- and supply-side variables. Furthermore, it may be overzealous to create a model for each physical homogeneous region as this ignores other regions that share all the identified characteristics that should, if appropriate, be integrated into a more complete model.

Nevertheless, stratification is generally performed manually, with attention given to *a priori* local knowledge. Adair and McGreal (1987), in their study of the Belfast residential property market, proposed that primary sub-markets should be formed for: Inner City; Middle City; Outer City; Greater East and South; Greater North; and Greater West. They also proposed that these sub-markets should then be further subdivided into terraced, semi-detached and detached.

Ranking location by average property value

One method of representing location is to include in the appraisal model average house prices for each location. This approach was taken by Jenkins (1992) where average values were fed from a database into an expert system in order to provide a surrogate for location.

The Glamorgan team later experimented with this approach for residential property data selected from the Cardiff area, using a neural network model. The results show a small increase in accuracy, most notably when average values were computed for house type within region. However, the relatively small increase in modelling accuracy suggests average value is not a sufficiently good surrogate. Yet, the approach is similar to that taken by many house buyers (and perhaps also estate agents) when assessing the relative 'value for money' of the subject property.

Coupling property data with regional statistics

To increase the modelling susceptibility of the data, it may be profitable to couple the property transaction data with other descriptive data sets. Data describing a region's wealth, employment, schools, air quality, weather, population, etc may prove useful as additional features to include in a model. Sources of such data include: market research, regional employment statistics, census of population, regional crime statistics, school league tables, pollution studies, electoral roll, television regions, credit-related data and others. The most structured and accessible of these are the data recorded by the UK Census of Population. This data is available in raw form and also as commercial geodemographic indicators that have been enhanced using market survey data (see Sleight, 1993).

Census data are available at a number of abstraction levels with the smallest being Enumeration District (ED) in England and Wales, and Output Area (OA) in Scotland. A coding system allows access keys to be generated by following a country/county/ district/ward/ED route. In addition to this a cross-reference from postcode to ED allows individual properties to be included in ED level statistics (Dale and Marsh, 1993).

Adair and McGreal (1987) used Census data to reflect a wide range of socio-economic characteristics relating to home-ownership levels, employment, population density and segregation by religion. Using MRA in a way that iteratively selects the most influential variables (stepwise regression), some of their final models included ward level Census aggregates and were deemed important in predicting property value.

One empirical study undertaken at Glamorgan, and described more fully elsewhere (see Lewis *et al* 1997), linked residential property data with Census data at the district and ED level using neural networks. Some improvement in accuracy was gained even at the very highest level of abstraction. However, as had been anticipated, the greatest gains occurred at the ED level, where the mean absolute percentage error was reduced from 20% (original data set) to 13% (original data and ED level Census statistics) for a randomly selected test set. The approach not only set a course toward the requirements of the first objective, but also, in embracing data that is traditionally beyond the scope of DCC, pointed the way toward partial satisfaction of the second objective (section 4.4).

Automated stratification

Almy *et al* (1998) suggest that stratification of markets should be a preliminary step for all computer-assisted mass appraisal (CAMA) systems. However, little attention has been paid to potential automation processes in valuation literature. This became a key focus for the research team and is described in the next section.

4.5.3 Empirical work

The first objective was to 'spread the net' so that data could be taken from across a whole city and achieve at least the same level of accuracy as MRAor neural network analysis in a single 'district'. It was presumed that city-wide data could be segmented by a neural network to reveal not one but many useful patterns. To use such a system to predict the value of a previously unseen property next requires a method of selecting the appropriate pattern (and its corresponding function). This required an extra step over the 'traditional' neural network approach.

In its first approach, the team used a clustering algorithm both to identify patterns within the parent dataset and to act as a panel judge to decide which function to select when asked to give a valuation. In a second approach a technique known as a genetic algorithm was adopted. (The Appendix describes these methods in some detail and reports the empirical work undertaken by Lewis.)

The results obtained using the clustering algorithm were encouraging (see Appendix, section A1.1). Initially, only the same sorts of supply-side data that valuers use in making comparisons were utilised. The team was able to take data at a city-wide level, identify many patterns in the dataset and increase prediction accuracy by 10% over the 'conventional' neural network approach. However, there were clear indications that further research would yield greater improvements, both in relation to identifying patterns and in relation to demand-side data.

Essentially, there were two main problems with the clustering algorithm:

- a weakness in identifying where one pattern finished and another began – in other words, detecting boundaries in the patterns was a real issue; and
- the fitness of the variables selected during the clustering process in producing useful training sets.

The proposed solution involves the use of genetic algorithms and the Gamma test. The Appendix, sections A1.2 and A1.3 describes these techniques and the detailed results obtained. What the studies clearly demonstrate is that:

- stratification is advantageous – valuation performance of ANNs is enhanced by stratifying a heterogeneous market;
- automating the stratification process can be achieved efficiently;

- valuation performance is enhanced by coupling demand-side data with the more traditional transaction data used by surveyors.

The Appendix describes the techniques as stand-alone entities, with performance comparisons made between them. This is a good way to assess their individual performance but not necessarily an effective way to use them. A strategy for amalgamating the output of each approach in a way that would select the 'optimal' overall result (or some measure of central tendency) would produce a tool that is of most benefit to a residential property valuer. Section 4.7 describes one means for achieving such an outcome.

The very mention of such complex, computer-based techniques will generate aversion in most GP surveyors and part of that aversion is a legitimate fear about intelligibility. In other words, in the attempt to satisfy the first two objectives of the research strategy – the utilisation of data from heterogeneous areas embracing demand- as well as supply-related variables – the team quickly heaped up problems with the third objective of intelligibility. That issue is addressed in the next section.

4.6 Developing intelligible systems

It is vitally important that any new method is acceptable to practitioners. This is particularly true of methods that are delivered on computer platforms. The software advert usually says that systems are cheap, easy to use, immensely powerful and, therefore, buying into them will improve efficiency, increase profits and dramatically reduce the golf handicap.

In fact, computing industry statistics suggest that 70% of all systems underperform. As much as 40% of all system development work is abortive because systems are not implemented. The chief causes of this failure to implement are:

- business cultures which are inimical to change;
- skilled incompetence – subtle resistance to change by practitioners; and
- insufficient training.

All three causes of failure have acceptability of new methods and technologies at their root. Acceptability requires an appropriate degree of understanding by the operators. It should be said at this stage that complete understanding is not the target. On the basis of what has been argued here, DCC would never be used if complete understanding were a prerequisite.

Indeed, on that basis other valuation paradigms would also prove difficult for many practitioners. For instance, the investment method of valuation requires an understanding of compounding and discounting functions. Many valuers are able to develop these functions from first principles and those that can very often embed such functions in spreadsheets of their own making.

However, some valuers struggle to build such functions. They look to textbooks for function descriptions, to valuation tables for arithmetic values to apply in calculations or to bespoke software.

Provided that the latter group knows when and how to apply functions, they suffer little disadvantage in comparison to the former group, at least in terms of routine performances. (The disadvantage becomes significant in the development of method.) What is the appropriate degree of understanding? One would prefer a surgeon to know why (s)he is doing what (s)he is doing. In his/her absence people will settle for a surgeon who knows how to do what (s)he is meant to.

If an intelligent alternative to DCC is to be used by appraisal professionals, some of them will be involved in building it from first principles. All must have a reasonable understanding of its processes, be confident in applying them and recognise when there is something wrong.

Of course the development of method described here is of a higher order than investment mathematics. The strategy discussed here is only possible because of the development of computer-aided techniques. The analogy with the surgical profession holds good. While surgeons are undoubtedly involved in the design of modern surgical tools, few surgeons understand the technologies that underpin them. Interestingly, the neural network is one of the techniques that are now also used in operating theatres, eg in analysing wounds that have been three-dimensionally scanned into computers.

Understanding breeds confidence. Those who use new systems will need to be confident in their use. They need to know the limits to which systems may be safely taken. They will also need reassurance about system suitability when the terrain changes. For this reason, intelligible systems will also need to communicate with users about the degree of confidence that is appropriate to any current transaction. Intelligibility requires that even if the calculation of confidence is regarded as complex by the user (eg it might utilise some variant of a conditional probability density function), nevertheless the communication of confidence to the user is simple to understand. This suggests that software is required that will shield the valuer from the complexity of the underlying models, that techniques will need to be embedded. The integration of what are still essentially research-based techniques into the everyday toolkit of the residential property valuer will require considerable ingenuity. The key will be the development of techniques that provide successful, reliable outcomes.

As well as this general sense in which systems need to be intelligible and acceptable to users, there is a more specific sense in which the methods described here need to offer intelligibility. In a court of law, or in a valuation tribunal, valuers are often called upon to explain the reasoning behind a decision. Because of the considerable commercial pressures on valuers described in earlier chapters, it is often the case that the original written valuation will cite comparable evidence but not elaborate on the analysis undertaken by the valuer. But whether a valuation report is adequately justified or some *ex post facto* rationalisation occurs, it is usually the case that a professional is able to construct a case to show reasonable performance.

In relation to some of the techniques described in this chapter, such a rationalisation is hidden from view. While the inputs to and outputs from a neural network may be identified, the inner workings of a network are not revealed. The network may be regarded as a 'black box'. Acceptability demands that the hidden processes are laid bare. The Appendix, section A2, describes the means identified to date at Glamorgan whereby the techniques under development might be 'opened up' to reveal 'reasoning' processes. However, it is recognised that, at this stage, explanation facilities remain primitive and that there is scope for further analysis of the extent to which human and machine processes may be reconciled. Indeed, further analysis of the decision-making processes used by valuers in DCC may well yield further material that assists such reconciliation.

The tension between the development of complex embedded techniques and the need for human understanding and control suggests a synthesis in some form of expert system interface. In such a synthesis, the interface will yield control of areas that demand human judgements to professional users. Interfaces to data will be transparent to users and permit human selection, but calculations once triggered will be largely hidden from view. The whole process must be audited automatically to leave a trail of the judgements taken.

4.7 Dealing with market cycles

A final issue for DCC and other techniques is the extent to which they can become predictive. Earlier it was noted that valuers have not developed time series analysis and literature on leading indicators is wanting. Given that some form of sustainable value would appear preferable to the measure of open market value, this is a serious deficiency that needs to be addressed.

There are many new mathematical ideas relating to time series, such as chaos theory, fractals, Takens' theorem and evolutionary techniques that may or may not be relevant to property data. The real estate research community needs to embrace and further investigate these techniques as applied to property. The Glamorgan team has recently embarked upon a new and specific phase of research.

If stratified neural network models can overcome the restrictions of earlier neural network approaches in relation to heterogeneous space within a relatively static time frame, it is postulated that similar results for time zones may be achieved in fixed spaces. An analogous approach using genetic algorithms and neural networks is under way with two objectives.

The initial objective is not predictive but rather seeks to identify appropriate valuation functions for particular time frames. This in itself would be very useful, as it would permit an analysis of the changing nature of appropriate functions over time and in the process identify permanent elements of such functions. The second objective would be to develop functions in relation to early data that attempted to predict values in later time frames, using approaches developed and explained by Vermuri and Rogers (1994).

In addition to such empirical work, an ongoing debate about the appropriate measure of value is necessary. Open market value or bid price clearly contain a perfectly legitimate speculative and 'emotional' (ie a premium paid to satisfy some subjective attachment) element. Estimated realisation price tends to put bids in some form of temporal perspective. But what violence is done to market efficiency if (theoretical) constraints are placed on speculative bidding? Should the speculative element of bids be cash-backed (rather than financed by long-term borrowing)? If desirable, how could this be implemented? There may already be sound answers to these questions, but for the author – and perhaps residential appraisers more generally – they remain to be discovered.

4.8 Dealing with arbitrariness

Most of the applied neural network research in property appraisal has tended to emphasise the positive. However, a stubborn strain[2] has consistently emphasised some negatives!

Lenk *et al* (1997) examined critically the efficacy of MRA and ANNs. They compared the predictive performance of a single MRA model with three ANNs with respect to their ability to estimate the value of a random sample of typical residential properties and a sample of outlier properties. The MRA model outperformed all three ANNs, corroborating the findings of Worzala *et al* (1995) who concluded that data issues might mitigate the consistent success of ANN models for real estate valuation.

The problems according to this school of thought are that:

- ANNs are not easy to use;
- results are inconsistent between ANN packages;
- results are inconsistent between runs of the same neural network software;
- ANNs can have very long run times.

Earlier research by Lu and Lu (1991) had already identified such disadvantages of neurocomputing and offered strategies to cope with them. A great deal of effort in research terms has since been required in order to identify:

- specific forms of ANNs that are suitable for the appraisal problem;
- problems in data preparation and optimal methods for dealing with them;
- problems with ANN 'settings' like learning rates and momentum.

Nevertheless, sufficient problems with stand-alone networks have persisted prompting respected commentators like McGreal to suggest a more sceptical approach (McGreal *et al* 1998). Such deficiencies are very real, though in the last half of the 1990s more thorough strategies have been developed to cope with the arbitrariness associated with ANN application.

Perhaps the most useful strategy has been labelled MANN – a Modular Artificial Neural Network (Haykin, 1994). Dr Panayiotou of the Lands and Surveys Department of the Government of

Cyprus has applied MANN strategy to the appraisal of houses and apartments for taxation purposes and suggests that the more sceptical approach advocated by McGreal is satisfied in the deployment of MANN (Panayiotou, 1999). (A description of Dr Panayiotou's modular artificial neural network system is outlined in the Appendix, section A3.)

Very few new techniques spring fully formed from the laboratory and the early cautious, measured optimism from Lu and Lu (1991) is worth repeating:

> What makes neurocomputing technology especially promising is the fact that this technology is just at the inception stage. The scope of neurocomputing will certainly be expanded rapidly...

4.9 Conclusions

The problem as defined in this book is that the traditional method is deficient and prone to periodic redundancy at key moments in the market cycle. This is reason enough to prompt serious investigation aimed at redressing the situation.

This chapter and the accompanying Appendix present an analysis of how several different techniques can be used to assist in residential appraisal. What needs to be made clear is that none of the proposed methods taken individually offers a solution. Taken together the various constituents suggest a refined traditional DCC approach and a supplementary neural statistical method that may one day qualify as an alternative.

Some years back a psychologist called Donald Schön attempted to hold back the tide of the prevailing technical rational epistemology of the postwar period. In its place he wanted to restore professional judgement as art. He began to raise serious issues about professional decision-making.

But the technophiles have quietly latched onto his insights to develop yet more rigorous specifications for truly intelligent systems. Knowledge engineers seem to be growing in capability and confidence.

Valuation judgement needs to be based on sound evidence and thorough analysis. This requires the development of tools and methods that embrace powerful new techniques. To the consternation of some that think on valuation as art, much of the initiative has emanated from the scientific community and is to be resisted. To the consternation of some that think on valuation as science, human judgement has held centre stage and is to be upstaged.

To those who think that science and art have been falsely counter-posed, who aim for methods that are at once sympathetic to the strengths of both, falls the task of reconciliation.

Notes

1   The contention here is that some measure of sustainable value is a sensible output when valuing for mortgage purposes.
2   Worzola *et al* (1995) and Lenk *et al* (1997) are two studies applied to real estate appraisal that emanate from Colorado State University. They confirm earlier caution about neural network models in finance-related fields from unpublished research by Allen and Zumwalt at the same institution in 1994.

References

Adair, A.S. and McGreal, W.S. (1987) 'The application of multiple regression analysis in property valuation', *Journal of Valuation*, 6, 57–67.

Adair, A. and McGreal, W.S. (1995) *Investigation of the Influence of Property and Socio-Economic Variables on Residential Values and the Formulation of Valuation Models Based on Regression Analysis.* Technical Report, Real Estate Studies Unit, School of the Built Environment, University of Ulster.

Adair, A.S., Berry, J.N. and McGreal, W.S. (1996) 'Hedonic modelling, housing submarkets and residential valuation', *Journal of Property Research*, 13, 67–83.

Almond, N.I., Jenkins, D.H. and Gronow, S.A. (1998) 'Development of a prototype residential valuation system', in *Computers in Urban Planning and Management*, Vol. 1. New Delhi and London: Narosa Publishing.

Almy, R., Horbas, J., Cusack, M., Gloudemans, R. (1997) 'The valuation of residential property using regression analysis' in McClusky, W.J. and Adair, A.S. (eds), *Computer Assisted Mass Appraisal: An International Review.* Aldershot: Ashgate Publishing.

Borst, R.A. (1991) 'Artificial neural networks: the next modelling/calibration technology for the assessment community?', *Property Tax Journal*, 10, 69–94.

Dale A., and Marsh, C. (1993) *The 1991 Census User's Guide.* London: Stationery Office.

Eckert, J.K. (1990) *Property Appraisal and Assessment Administration.* Chicago: International Association of Assessing Officers.

Evans, A., James, H. and Collins, A. (1992) 'Artificial neural networks: an application to residential valuation in the UK', *Journal of Property Valuation and Investment*, 11, 195–204.

Greaves, M. (1984) 'The determinants of residential values: the hierarchical and statistical approaches', *Journal of Valuation*, 3, 5–23.

Gronow, S. and Scott, I. (1985) 'Expert systems', *Estates Gazette*, 276, 1012–14.

Have, G.M. ten, Veld, A.G. op't, Janssen, J.E. (1997) 'TAXES: residential property valuation for local tax purposes in the Netherlands', in McClusky, W.J. and Adair, A.S. (eds), *Computer Assisted Mass Appraisal: An International Review*. Aldershot: Ashgate Publishing.

Haykin, S. (1994) *Neural Networks: A Comprehensive Foundation*. New York and Oxford: Macmillan College Publishing, pp. 1–41, 473–95.

Honey, R. (1997) *The Impact of IT on the Property Industry*. London: RICS.

International Association of Assessing Officers (1978) *Improving Real Property Assessment: AReference Manual*. Chicago: IAAO.

James, H. (1994) *An 'Automatic Pilot' for Surveyors*, Cutting Edge Conference. London: RICS.

Jenkins D.H. (1992) 'Expert systems in the land strategy of Cardiff City Council.' Unpublished MPhil thesis, Polytechnic of Wales.

Jenkins, D.H., Gronow, S. and Prescott, G. (1989) 'Information technology: the changing nature of local government property management', *Property Management*, 8(1), 75–88.

Lenk, M.M., Worzala, E.M. and Silva, A. (1997), 'High-tech valuation: should artificial neural networks bypass the human valuer?', *Journal of Property Valuation and Investment*, 15(1), 8–26.

Lewis, O., Ware, A. and Jenkins, D.H. (1997) 'A novel neural network technique for modelling data containing multiple functions', in Reusch, Bernd (ed.), *Computational Intelligence – Theory and Applications*, Lecture Notes in Computer Science Series Vol. 1226. London and New York: Springer-Verlag.

Lu, M. and Lu, D. (1991) 'Neurocomputing approach to residential property valuation', *Journal of Microcomputer Systems Management*, 4(2), 21–9.

McGreal, W.S., Adair, A.S., McBurney, D. and Patterson, D. (1998) 'Neural networks: the prediction of residential values', *Journal of Property Valuation and Investment*, 16(1), 55–70.

Panayiotou, P.A. (1999) 'Immovable property taxation and the development of an ANN valuation system of residential properties for tax purposes in Cyprus.' Unpublished PhD thesis, University of Glamorgan.

Sauter, B. (1985) *Solving Today's Computer Assisted Valuation Issues Using the Adaptive Estimation Procedure and Bayesian Regression*. Paper presented at the Second World Congress on Computer Assisted Valuation, Lincoln Institute of Land Policy, Massachusetts.

Sleight, P. (1993) *Targeting Customers: How to Use Geodemographic and Lifestyle Data in Your Business*. Henley-on-Thames: NTC Publications.

Strazheim, M.R. (1973) 'Estimation of the demand for urban housing services from interview data', *Review of Economics and Statistics*, 55, 1–8.

Vermuri, S. and Rogers, Y. (1994) *Artificial Neural Networks Forecasting Time Series*. CA: IEEE Computer Society Press.

Wiltshaw, D.G. (1991) 'Valuation by comparable sales and linear algebra', *Journal of Property Research*, 8, 3–19.

Worzola, E., Lenk, M. and Silva, A. (1995) 'An exploration of neural networks and its application to real estate valuation', *Journal of Real Estate Research*, 10(2), 185–201.

Chapter 5

Public-Sector Residential Valuations

5.1 Overview

Heretofore the concern has been for properties traded in the open market where asking prices are suggested by estate agents and professional valuers verify bid prices. In this chapter consideration is given to some instances in which public-sector houses are valued or where privately owned residential assets are valued for public-sector purposes. Section 5.2 considers the valuation of assets under 'Right To Buy' legislation. Section 5.3 examines council tax valuations, while section 5.4 explores the valuations of residential assets held by the public sector.

5.2 The 'Right To Buy' valuation

The 'Right To Buy' legislation gave tenants of public-sector housing the right to acquire the property in which they resided (a qualification period was deemed appropriate). This type of valuation is of interest primarily because the legislation required that the sale price be calculated at open market value less a discount that related to the length of qualifying tenancy. Hence the calculation was a modified form of open market valuation. (There were and are a variety of other qualifications related to the price, eg the price could not be less than the cost of provision for recently constructed houses.)

Launched in 1980, the scheme was well received. Tenants in some instances were able to buy properties on terms cheaper than continued rental. Some of the public-sector stock was quite attractive. In some areas, local authorities had acquired private-sector housing for rehabilitation. In semi-rural areas, workers' cottages were particularly attractive. Sometimes, small-scale development in or adjacent to private-sector estates had taken place.

These properties sold well and, more to the point here, were readily assimilated into private markets. From a valuer's perspective, the properties were marketable and some comparable data from the private sector was reasonably adapted to vindicate valuation decisions.

The real valuation difficulty concerned properties for which there had been no market traditionally and which would require a critical mass of sales before viable markets were established. This included much housing that had been constructed on large-scale estates.

Initial valuations proved troublesome. Some comparisons were possible with properties at the lower end of the private sector, though quite often the accommodation standards of the public-sector stock were better.[1]

Valuers adopted various forms of 'beacon' approach where new cases were repeatedly valued by reference to earlier transactions typifying strata of the stock. In calculating dispersion around such beacon values, some valuers made reference to cost differentials.[2]

Tenants were given a right to appeal against the decisions of local authorities, the agencies that had erstwhile managed the stock (who either contracted the valuation work out to estate agents/ valuers or built up in-house teams). Appeals were allowed against these valuations to the District Valuation Office of the Inland Revenue. Most appeals were upheld and valuations reduced (though the basis was not made clear and valuers often suspected that a policy to promote sales was being operated).

The appeals decisions became the new beacons – benchmark 'comparables' for the conduct of other valuations. The tone was set for the whole 'market' and it became possible to create a quasi-science in which whole sub-'markets' could be compared and attributes could be 'priced'. In more than one local authority, valuers took to using formulae that paid attention to Inland Revenue appeals data and attribute data. In fact the homogeneity of council housing stock made them a particularly fertile environment for the application of statistical approaches and the development of computerised techniques.

When stock found its way back on to the market, the accuracy of the earlier valuations was open to review and such transaction data naturally became the focus for comparable analysis. When this data and the outcomes of Right To Buy legislation is examined in terms of housing markets, the relevance of valuations in this sector to the more general propositions concerning valuation theory in this book can be articulated.

The Right To Buy legislation has been a great success in terms of initial policy objectives. Almost 30% of tenants have acquired houses. For most purchasers the experience has been a positive one. Asset values have increased greatly and deeply discounted prices (averaging 50% of assessed values) have brought high levels of security for the more stable, affluent tenants for whom purchase was an attractive option.

This positive account is partial in that it fails to report on the consequences in those regions, localities and estates in which the Right To Buy did not prove quite so popular.[3] The serious social crises of disintegration and exclusion are concentrated in areas of poorer, unsold (or bought-back) housing stock. In such areas, the young unemployed live in close proximity to those too old to have taken advantage of the Right To Buy. These estates are rapidly decaying and, in areas where the labour market seems unlikely to recover, are being considered for partial and sometimes wholesale demolition.

The significance of the valuation issues is small in relation to the larger issues that frame it, but should be stated. While valuers' attention was correctly addressed to supply-side issues of design, layout, materials and environment, these factors must necessarily be placed in the 'demand context'. Physical variability within the council stock is far less than the private sector; even so, there are quite dramatic socio-economic differences within neighbourhoods and between regions. The quality of housing is far less important than valuers appeared to think. Zero demand means zero value.

In the peak year of 1982 thousands of council houses in many urban areas were valued at around £20,000. Within conurbations there were slight variations to account for location, materials, design and accommodation. Some of these houses, identical in almost all respects, are valued in the year 2000 in excess of £50,000, while others may have a value as public open space less the cost of demolition.

Some may argue that the valuations were correct at the time but that would be to miss the point. While it would have been difficult to predict future movements in value or to assess, for example, which estates were likely to achieve a threshold of sales that would make for sustainable and viable markets, no such predictions or assessments were contemplated.

At key moments in the valuation of social housing under the Right To Buy scheme, the comparative process had very little to offer. By failing to examine demand-side attributes explicitly, where the comparative process was able to offer some support it did so in a clumsy and inefficient way. Cost-based and formulaic approaches probably fared no worse.

Tax band	Value range (£k)	Proportion
A	0–40	6
B	40–52	7
C	52–68	8
D	68–88	9
E	88–120	11
F	120–160	13
G	160–320	15
H	320+	18

Figure 5.1 Council tax bands. For example, if a £35,000 house attracts council tax of £180, a house of twice that value will attract tax of £270 (Band D)

5.3 Council tax valuations

The council tax is a means of raising local authority revenue. Introduced in April 1993 the tax is based on the capital value of domestic property in the open market as at 1 April 1991 and is levied on occupiers of properties according to the tax 'band' in which the value of the property falls. Figure 5.1 shows the tax bands for England and the proportion of tax payable within each property band. The rate of tax is locally determined.

The valuation exercise raised eyebrows in professional circles because there was no detailed survey of properties – not even of beacon properties. The valuation proceeded on the basis of the most cursory inspection of neighbourhoods and adopted the notion of beacon values of representative properties from which the values of neighbouring properties were imputed. This represented a highly condensed form of the comparative process! The average cost of valuation was £1.60 per property.

This was an interesting exercise in that the traditional issue of accuracy in valuation was literally marginalised. Accuracy became an issue at the margins of bands. Unsurprisingly there were many appeals – close to 1 million – and the administrative cost of appeals actually exceeded the cost of valuation. However, given the initial low valuation cost and that there were 21 million properties assessed, the exercise was unsurprisingly judged as a success by the National Audit Office (1994). The more important consideration for local property taxes is that they are fair and seen to be fair and a report by the Joseph Rowntree Foundation in the same year concluded that the fairness criterion had also been met (Travers and Kneen, 1994).

Given that the tax seems to have been introduced cheaply and fairly, it might be supposed that there was little else to say. However, a number of commentators have suggested reform in recent years (see for example Plimmer *et al* 1999). The thrust of criticism is that given the fixed valuation date equity is impaired with the passage of time and that regressivity is present. The suggested remedies are periodic revaluation of properties and a reform of the banding system (IRRV, 1998).

Furthermore, not all wrongly banded properties were appealed. Given the high variability in value within neighbourhoods, it comes as no surprise to see National Audit Office (1994) estimates that in all probability only 76% of all dwellings were correctly banded – leaving a substantial 24% or 5 million properties in the wrong band. Given the bandwidths, this is a high figure and leaves one guessing about the number of properties wrongly valued within bands.

Other commentators have suggested alternative approaches to valuation method. Indeed most of the alternative valuation methods discussed in this book, including MRA, neural networks and geographic information systems, have been mooted as appropriate means of valuation at some time or another and in some instances actually applied to council tax data experimentally (see Longley *et al* 1993).

The obvious difference between mortgage valuation and council tax valuation is that the target output is no longer a point (eg £25,500) but a class (eg Band A). This allows the development of a classification rather than a regression-based appraisal model. Neural networks are as well suited – if not more suited – to classification problems, and there are also alternative 'artificial intelligence' techniques that could be employed such as tree induction algorithms. One member of the Glamorgan team undertook a comparison of MRA, ANN and tree induction algorithms to estimate council tax bands (see Lewis, 1999).

ANN implementation outperformed the tree induction and the MRA model for a test set but notably the tree induction algorithm fared considerably better when predicting the council tax band for a training set (due to the fact that tree induction techniques learn examples within the training set compared with ANN models that learn general underlying patterns). The notable advantage that tree induction techniques have over ANNs is their ability to explicitly reveal the structure of the generated model. Specifically, tree induction techniques can be read as 'expert system' rules.

This is a fertile area for the application and development of new techniques that hold the potential to utilise more and better quality data and produce more rigorous results. It would even seem sensible for the various interested professional organisations to establish some benchmark data against which the usefulness and accuracy of various proposed alternative methods might be measured.

5.4 Asset valuations of social housing

Despite the success of the Right To Buy legislation, 16% of UK property (3.3 million houses) is still owned and managed by local authorities. The decline in local authority stock has been roughly matched in recent times by the growth in stock (1 million dwellings) of registered social landlords (RSLs). Mostly housing associations (but also co-operatives, charitable trusts and local housing companies), RSLs, like local authorities, offer properties at subsidised rents.

The triggers for valuation in this sector include:

- the large-scale voluntary transfer of stock from local authorities to RSLs;[4]
- the valuation of RSL stock for a lender considering a loan on the security of those assets;[5] and
- stock valuation for local authorities for the new resource accounting regulations.[6]

The bases of valuation include existing use value for social housing (EUV-SH), separately defined within the RICS Red Book, and open market value (subject to tenancy). These valuation bases require the use of investment valuation techniques and are therefore beyond the scope of this book. The most sensitive inputs to the valuation are permissible rates of rental growth (government determined), the rate of cost inflation and a discount rate that is also strongly influenced by government. Comparability is barely an issue given the paucity of market transactions.

However, two issues of interest are raised in the context of stock valuation for resource accounting by local authorities, namely:

- the proposed extension of the 'beacon' principle; and
- the method of establishing EUV-SH by reference to vacant possession values (EUV-VP) from comparison with evidence of house sales, including council house sales. The EUV-VP is subsequently adjusted (by reference to regionally based adjustment factors) to reflect occupation by a secure tenant to establish EUV-SH.

The proposed guidance on the stock valuation defines the beacon principle and beacon values in some depth and elaborates key stages in the application of the beacon approach.

What is of particular note is that in pursuit of the EUV-VP the guidance establishes the requirement to record:

- minimum numbers of comparable sales upon which the beacon valuation has been based;
- explicit adjustments to the sales evidence to fit the beacon property;
- the application of the adjusted sales evidence to the beacon property to provide the beacon valuation;
- the quality of comparable data – this is particularly emphasised in relation to property where an owner-occupied market is absent or construction is unusual.

Such standards are equivalent to those suggested more generally by the Glamorgan team in relation to the discharge of obligations when valuing a property for mortgage purposes by DCC.

Expert database systems developed by the author (particularly that for the valuation of Cardiff City Council's residential portfolio in 1988) are well suited to such valuations, though the various techniques commonly deployed in computer-assisted mass appraisal, including newer approaches like MANN and GIS, could readily be marshalled for such purposes.

Notes

1 Confirmed by the fact that ex-council stock sometimes represents a step up from the bottom of the market.
2 Clearly current costs of provision were very often much higher than anything likely to be achieved in the open market (reflecting the high degree of subsidy in relation to such assets) but cost was a useful surrogate in measuring dispersion.

3 I do not mean by this to attribute these problems to the legislation. Large-scale abandonment of public-sector housing, for example, was known in the UK prior to 1980.
4 Between its introduction in 1988 and the summer of 1999, 86 authorities had transferred all or part of their assets to RSLs (DETR, 1999a).
5 Regulated under PS10 of the RICS Red Book.
6 At the time of writing, the government was still consulting regarding the guidance of valuation (see DETR, 1999b) for the new regulations (see DETR, 1998).

References

DETR (1998) *A New Financial Framework for Local Authority Housing: Resource Accounting in the Housing Revenue Account*, December.

DETR (1999a) *Housing Transfers in England Dealing with Overhanging Debt and Altering the LSVT Levy*, August.

DETR (1999b) *Guidance on Stock Valuation for Resource Accounting*, November.

IRRV (1998) *Response to DETR Consultation Paper on Improving Local Financial Accountability*, London.

Lewis, O.M. (1999) 'The use of artificial intelligence techniques to assist in the valuation of residential properties.' Unpublished PhD thesis, University of Glamorgan.

Longley, P., Higgs, G. and Martin, D. (1993) 'A GIS based appraisal of council tax valuations', *Journal of Property Valuation and Investment*, Computer Briefing, 11(4), 375–83.

National Audit Office (1994) *The Valuation Office Agency: Council Tax Valuation in England and Wales.* London: HMSO.

Plimmer, F., McCluskey, W.J., Connellan, O. (1999) 'Reform of UK local government domestic property taxes', *Property Management*, 17(4), 336–52.

Travers and Kneen [*sic*] (1994) *Estates Gazette*, 9422, 60.

Chapter 6

Conclusions

6.1 Brief overview

Residential appraisal is by far the largest activity undertaken by chartered surveyors. However, there has been no specific training or qualification for the task. Current practice lacks rigour and regulation.

If the purpose of residential mortgage appraisal is to answer one question, 'does the asset offer adequate security for a loan?' – a question of interest to both lender and consumer – then observations of practice suggest a quite radical disjuncture between the normative approach and the actual approach of practitioners. Of particular note are the following points:

- The actual approach to appraisal estimates the 'open market value'. This measure of value approached using the traditional method (DCC in this text) reflects bid prices at points on the price curve when the sensible measure would relate to sustainable value, shorn of speculative and emotional elements.
- The review in Chapters 2 and 3 of the development of the market for the supply of appraisal advice demonstrated how structural factors have influenced the distortion of the 'traditional method'.
- DCC as a legitimate heuristic in approaching value has been compromised by current practice. Key stages in the traditional method are routinely omitted.
- DCC is tightly constrained as a method by lack of public data in regard to market transactions and by the neglect of demand-side data.
- In any case, DCC has inherent weaknesses that suggest sole reliance on it is socially and economically unsafe. This weakness is most clearly demonstrated in the wake of cyclical peaks and troughs.

These observations do not amount to a denial of the legitimacy of DCC as a valuation method. However, DCC may be less suitable than alternatives when appraisal is required to identify sustainable values.

For lenders still requiring opinions of the risk associated with lending decisions, alternative methods like those identified in Chapter 4 and the Appendix are appropriate.

However, the purpose of residential appraisal as defined does not fully meet with the objective interests of the consumer. A second question should be: 'Am I receiving value for money in this market if I purchase the property at this price?' In order to answer this question it is quite possible that a traditional DCC approach to open market value is valid, provided that the methodological and practical weaknesses identified are addressed and that in particular more consideration is given than customary to future trends. Again, the methods outlined in Chapter 4 could become a useful tool provided that they can be made intelligible.

In concluding Chapter 2 it was suggested that DCC is analogous to the method of personnel recruitment that was used prior to the development of psychometric and other testing methods. The key question in relation to the alternatives suggested is whether they have risen above the equivalent of phrenology! Hopefully, some readers will be willing to find out.

6.2 Summary of recommendations

The following recommendations have been made by researchers at Glamorgan for consideration by professional bodies and government agencies.

- Action is required regarding the dilution of method in the appraisal stage of the valuation. A code of practice should be drawn up to ensure that acceptable methods are being followed, not unlike the draft guidance produced for social housing accounting.
- A more rigorous approach to demand-side data should be promoted with mandatory recording of key demand-side variables.
- There should be a local licensing system to ensure that practitioners are competent to perform in an area. This licensing should be independent of vested interests.
- The specific education and training of housing appraisal should be put in hand with due weight given to the use of new techniques.
- A national database of all house transactions should be independently maintained and accessible to licensed practitioners.
- The measure of value – OMV – should be reviewed. Spot prices are hardly suitable for measuring sustainable value.

- The market should be regulated to ensure that consumers receive independent advice. There is no longer a coincidence of interest between lenders and borrowers.
- Refinements to the DCC approach should be fostered to take advantage of the latest developments in intelligent database technology.
- The development of supplementary methods of appraisal and forecasting should be promoted.

Appendix

Overview

This appendix describes in more detail some of the processes alluded to in Chapter 4. It is designed for those who wish to pursue further the strategy outlined earlier. Dr Owen Lewis undertook the empirical work described in sections A1 and A2, while Dr Panayiotis Panayiotou authored the work outlined in section A3.

Section A1 describes the new automated methods used to 'break' larger markets into more manageable sub-markets. Section A2 discusses the intelligibility problem that is seen as a major drawback to the use of 'neural' statistics by professional practices. Section A3 reports on the development of a MANN system designed to circumvent the problem of arbitrariness associated with neural network applications to appraisal problems.

A1 Modelling a heterogeneous market

Before considering approaches for automating the stratification process, it is useful to develop a visual interpretation of the role of sub-markets in a heterogeneous market. Figure A1 provides a purely abstract view of the interplay of sub-market functions in a heterogeneous market: here a heterogeneous market is viewed as a conceptual mathematical (not geographic) space containing many functions accounting for the observed sub-market behaviour.

The theoretical aim of any stratification process is then to segment this multifunctional space into smaller sub-regions containing a single value function. The first approach adopted used 'clustering' techniques (section A1.1), the second approach used genetic algorithms (section A1.2) and the abilities of both were subsequently tested using the Gamma test (section A1.3).

A1.1 Stratification using clustering techniques

Geodemographic indicators could be employed to describe sub-regions in a heterogeneous residential area. Those sub-regions

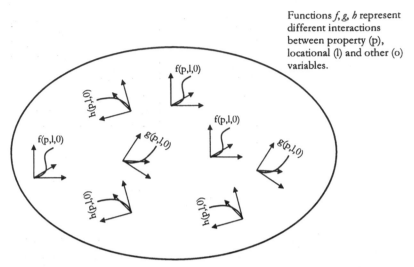

Heterogeneous residential property market

Figure A1 Abstract interpretation of functions in a heterogeneous property market described in a mathematical conceptual space

sharing the same characteristics could be grouped into a single model based on the assumption that similar areas have similar underlying value functions. Extending this reasoning, clusters found in Census data may correlate with homogeneous regions with respect to location, and clusters found in property data may describe homogeneous regions of properties. Early work by James (1994) concluded that an unsupervised neural network might be able to discern groupings within a parent data set that might represent homogenous areas.

Using an unsupervised neural network

An unsupervised network, such as the Kohonen network, organises itself in such a way as to represent classes within a data set. The 2-D Kohonen network allows classes to be visualised on a feature map, in which similar inputs are spatially clustered. Figure A2 shows a typical 2-D Kohonen self-organising map (SOM) along with an abridged algorithm. (Note that the number of nodes is arbitrarily selected for example purposes.)

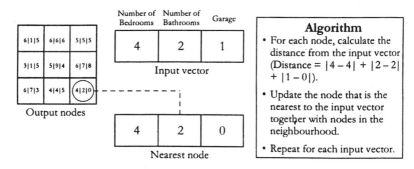

Figure A2 A Kohonen self-organising feature map

Each output node on the Kohonen feature map contains a vector of length 'j', where 'j' is equal to the number of input attributes. Before training the network is in an initialised state (ie the directions of the vectors in each node are random). Training involves passing an input vector into the network through the input nodes. Each node on the Kohonen feature map is then compared with the input vector, and the closest node is then changed to be more like the input vector. Neighbouring nodes also become more like the input vector. Iterating this process achieves clustering of similar input vectors in Euclidean space. Each observed cluster generated by the Kohonen SOM is used to train a single multi-layer perceptron (MLP) network as shown in Figure A3.

The novelty of this approach is in its ability to estimate the trainability of each cluster using the Gamma test (Stefánsson et al 1997).[1] This permits only 'useful' clusters to form training sets for MLP networks.

In order to provide a benchmark for analysing the methodology, a single MLP network was also trained on the whole data set. After training, the ability of the network to appraise residential properties with known values was tested. The results are shown in Table A1.

From the results obtained, it is evident that the methodology compares very favourably with the more 'conventional' neural network approach; the predictions made using the new method were 10% closer to the values returned by the valuer. This technique was also used to find clusters in Census data. This was achieved by using the Census variables as the training data for a Kohonen SOM. Results show an improvement in accuracy of between 1% and 14% using the sub-models over the single-model benchmark.

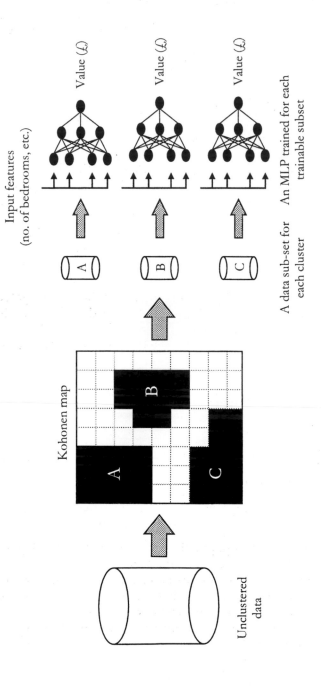

Figure A3 The Kohonen map produces clusters that are subsequently trained using MLPs

Table A1 Results obtained from clustering property types

	Conventional method	Kohonenn method
Mean absolute % error	18%	8%
% of records with error >10%	74%	22%
Minimum mean absolute % error	0%	0%
Maximum mean absolute % error	310%	49%

The disadvantage with this method relates to the estimation of trainability post clustering. If care is not taken when choosing variables to use as inputs to the Kohonen map, then a high proportion of the clusters will not be suitable as training sets. For example, if a cluster relates to the variable 'FrontDoorColour = White' then this will of course be unlikely to describe homogeneous properties. Although an absurd example, the reliance on *a priori* knowledge and post-clustering fitness testing must be noted.

To overcome this problem, the research team then investigated a further technique that permits fitness testing during clustering. This method recodes the market segmentation problem as a combinatorial one, before using genetic algorithms to produce homogeneous sub-sets.

A1.2 Stratification by genetic algorithm

Genetic algorithms (GAs) simulate the Darwinian theory of evolution (see Goldberg, 1989, for a good introduction to GAs). A typical GA operates at the level of genetic coding: the chromosomes or genotypes. Genotypes are usually simple bit strings of fixed length; the related 'adult' individuals (phenotypes) are obtained by decoding such bit strings using domain information. The basic steps of a typical genetic algorithm are as follows:

1   Randomly generate a population of individuals (bit strings).
2   Decode each individual and evaluate its fitness.
3   Generate a new population using cloning (survival of current individuals), cross-over (bit string reproduction) and mutation (random changing of bits in current individuals).
4   Repeat steps 2 and 3 until convergence (or another stopping condition is reached).

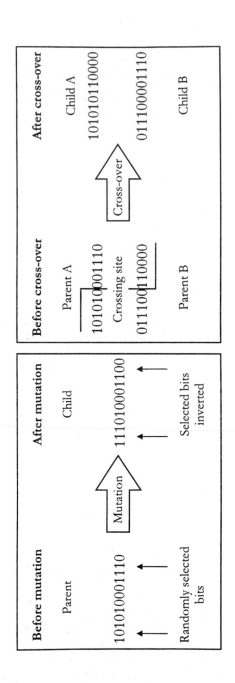

(a)

(b)

Figure A4 (a) A schematic of simple mutation showing the inversion of randomly selected bits. (b) A schematic of simple cross-over showing the partial exchange of information, using a crossing site chosen at random

Mutation and cross-over operators

The cross-over and mutation operators are fundamental to the development of a GA solution, from its random initial state to a near optimal mature state. In most GA applications, the encoding permits the use of standard mutation operators (random inversion of bits in a chromosome) and standard single or multiple cut cross-over operators. Figure A4 illustrates the effect of applying a mutation operator (a) and a single cut cross-over operator (b).

Binary coding of the 1991 Census data

The GA approach benefits from having binary representations of the domain data. The first step taken to achieve a binary representation for the 1991 Census data was to form a discrete representation of the raw data by normalising between 0 and 100. Each Census feature then represents percentage households or percentage persons in each Enumeration District (ED).

The discrete representations can then be converted to binary representations by setting thresholds and using values of True (1) if the subject value is below the threshold and False (0) otherwise. Figure A5 (a) and (b) give examples of a Census variable split into two and three partitions respectively.

Splitting each Census feature in this way allows a binary value to be used for each partition. For example, in the case of the two partitions, an ED that has a value below the 'Low' threshold can be represented as [1,0,0], with mid and high value EDs as [0,1,0] and [0,0,1] respectively.

Decoding and state evaluation

Chromosome decoding is required after each new generation has been created, in order to fix probabilities for survival (compete or partial) in later life. Decoding is relatively simple in this application with each $(n-1)$ bits (where n is the number of partitions) representing a single Census variable. EDs that satisfy a chromosome description can be identified, and residential properties within the selected EDs can be grouped and placed into a separate data set. State evaluation involves applying the Gamma test to the described data set and the appropriate metric(s) recorded. However, to speed up this process an initial pass of the Census data set is performed before the GA is run. The Census variables associated with each ED

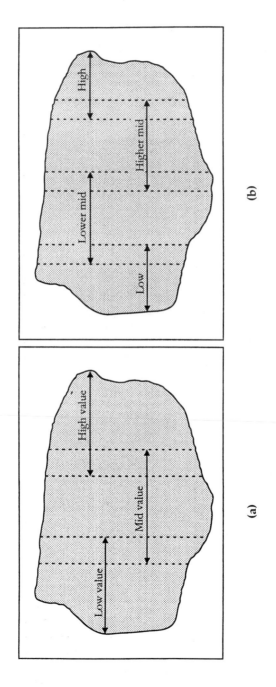

Figure A5 (a) Two soft partitions (b) Three soft partitions

	A B C D E F G	
	123123123123123123123	Seven variables (A...F) divided into three groups using two soft partitions.
ED string	100010001100010001100	Chromosome matches ED string
Chromosome	100010001100010001100	exactly so ED is selected.
ED string	100010001100010001100	Chromosome matches ED for each Census variable except where chromosome string is
Chromosome	111010001100010000100	[1,1,1] or [0,0,0]. Hence, ED is selected.
ED string	100010001100010001100	Chromosome does not match ED
Chromosome	100010001101010000100	string so ED is not selected.

Figure A6 Illustration of partial chromosome/ED matching used to select EDs on the basis of the current GA solution

Table A2 Results obtained for Census variable groupings using the described methodology

Census variable type	Single model %	Sub-model %	Improvement %
Whole data-set	20.57	–	–
Residents' age	24.78	14.05	10.73
	22.66	16.69	5.97
	23.88	14.89	8.99
	19.89	17.73	2.16
	19.78	18.3	1.48
Economic position	20.53	20.24	0.29
	20.65	20.25	0.45
	20.60	20.84	−0.24
	20.77	21.28	−0.51
	20.80	20.07	0.73
Amenities	19.23	12.68	6.55
	21.94	21.70	0.24
	21.68	21.95	−0.27
	22.23	23.10	−0.87
Car availability	19.75	15.52	4.23
	19.42	15.65	3.77
	19.95	14.32	5.63
	18.11	12.20	5.91
	22.41	16.24	6.17
Tenure	22.94	20.35	2.59
	17.63	14.72	2.91
	25.16	20.35	4.81
	25.19	20.00	5.19
	25.07	19.62	5.45
Working parents	19.82	13.01	6.81
	19.81	12.56	7.25
	20.77	21.13	−0.36
Profession	20.54	16.36	4.18
	19.78	15.62	4.16
	20.52	16.65	3.87
	27.60	12.26	15.34
	26.49	10.23	16.26
House type	21.45	14.64	6.81
	21.58	20.55	1.03
	21.06	14.80	6.26
	22.79	8.29	14.5
	21.49	17.15	4.34
Ethnic	21.45	21.64	0.19
	21.58	20.95	−0.63
Migration	19.35	19.99	0.64
	21.03	21.12	0.09
Travel to work	23.04	23.56	0.52

Table A3 Results obtained using a selection of Census variables

Description	Single model %	Sub-model %	Improvement %
Mixed selection 1	28.42	14.57	13.85
Mixed selection 2	18.05	15.57	2.48
Etc	30.14	16.05	14.09
	29.25	15.90	13.35
	20.17	18.92	1.25
	19.48	18.78	0.7

are converted into a binary representation using the described technique. Individual EDs can then be selected during the GA run by matching binary strings ignoring any [1,1,1] and [0,0,0] substrings in the current generation. Figure A6 provides examples of this partial matching technique between chromosomes and EDs.

Results

Table A2 shows the results obtained using the described methodology for each variable grouping. The mean absolute percentage error is shown for models trained on 'sub-market' data and also for the same data using a single MLP model. Any improvement in modelling accuracy is also shown.

Table A3 gives the results obtained when a selection of Census variables from different groupings were combined and used to generate sub-models.

The results indicate an overall improvement in modelling accuracy for the sub-model approach compared to the single-model approach. Looking first at the single Census group models, the largest individual improvements are observed for: Profession; House type; Car availability; and Residents' age models. Significant improvements were also made in Tenure and Working parent sub-models. However, somewhat surprisingly, no improvement was achieved using Economic position sub-models.

Although this type of selective analysis is of some benefit in ascertaining underlying model parameters, it is more probable that a neighbourhood description encompasses more than just one geodemographic feature grouping. Table A3 presents the results obtained from the genetic algorithm analysis using a broad range of Census variables. Here, the accuracy for the sub-models is fairly consistent (average 16.5%) showing an average improvement in accuracy of 7.5% compared with the single-model approach.

A1.3 The Gamma test

This phase in the research programme began by considering the use of Census data as additional features in an MLP network. Results show an increase in accuracy of 7% over the model containing just property attributes for the selected test set. However, this improvement in accuracy was not seen universally for the whole data set and can be partly attributed to the inability of the MLP network to model the complex multifunctional heterogeneous space.

Moreover, it was felt that this problem would persist if the Census data were replaced by up-to-date geodemographic data. What was required was a means of estimating the modelling capabilities of a data set.

The technique employed to estimate the susceptibility of the data to be modelled was the Gamma test. Based on a nearest-neighbour approach, this method gives a measure of both noise (intercept) and complexity (gradient), assuming that a single smooth continuous function underpins the data set. A number of assumptions can therefore be made about a set of data given its Gamma results. Firstly, a data set with a high noise value may have insufficient examples or descriptive features, or contain data mapped by multiple underlying functions. Assumptions can also be made based on the complexity value: a very complex underlying function may in fact be an aggregate of multiple functions which may be too complex for MLP or MRA to model.

The Gamma test was used to measure the homogeneity of the sub-sets generated by both of the stratification strategies described above, first the Kohonen SOM that had been used to cluster Census data, and secondly the genetic algorithm approach.

It will be remembered that Census aggregates were passed as input vectors to a Kohonen SOM, which clusters data according to their cross-characteristic similarities. After training, each cluster represented a set of residential properties linked via an enumeration to a postcode cross-reference look-up table. The Gamma test was used to estimate the trainability of each subset, those with low noise and low complexity forming training sets for individual MLP networks. The results show that the accuracy of the sub-models outperformed a single MLP control model within the range of 1% to 14%, with an average increase in modelling accuracy of 5%.

Although these result are promising, the generation of suitable training sets relies heavily upon selection of useful neighbourhood characteristics. Poor selection leads to clusters forming that perform badly when analysed by the Gamma test. This method is therefore of most use when *a priori* knowledge is available to determine the neighbourhood descriptors to select.

To overcome this dependence on *a priori* feature selection, a genetic algorithm was investigated. The GA generates a number of data sub-sets and the Gamma algorithm tests their fitness. Those sub-sets (or at least very similar ones) that fare the best are more likely to appear in successive generations. This process is iterated for a number of generations to produce an elite population, formed from data sub-sets with the best Gamma results. After termination, the elite sub-sets are used to train individual MLP networks in the same manner as the Kohonen SOM approach.

Here, the results are more consistent than the Kohonen approach as fitness is tested en route as opposed to post-clustering. An average increase in accuracy of 7.5 was observed, within a range of 0–16%.

A2 Intelligibility of the models

The ability to furnish users with explanations of the reasoning process or underlying functionality is an important feature of any model (Clancy, 1983). Explanation facilities are required, both for user acceptance and the validation of reasoning procedure (Davis *et al* 1977). This is a difficult task when analysing neural networks as they do not have explicit or 'declarative knowledge' (Diederich, 1989). As a result of the numeric and distributed nature of neural networks, any rules extracted directly from their internal structure are often 'unintelligible to the human' (Tay and Ho, 1992). Hence, neural networks are often described as being 'black box' in nature.

The internal workings of a neural network are, for the most part, hidden from the user. For a residential property valuer, this leads to a situation where one problem is solved, only for another to be created. A house may be valued accurately using neural network techniques, yet there is no explanation as to why or how the value was reached, thus the valuation is not defensible in a court of law or valuation tribunal.

An emerging branch of artificial intelligence research is tackling this very problem at a generic level. The aim is to replace where possible the parts of the neural network system that lack cognitive

Table A4 Example rules extracted from Kohonen SOM model

Seek Appropriate_Model

IF Percentage_Detached_Properties is inRange(0, 52)
AND Mean_&_Median (Detached, 21, 21)
AND 1st_&_3rd_Quartiles (Detached, 3, 35)
AND Percentage_SemiDetached_Properties is inRange(0, 48)
AND Mean_&_Median (SemiDetached, 21, 21)
AND 1st_&_3rd_Quartiles (SemiDetached, 12, 29)
AND Percentage_Terraced_Properties is inRange (0, 60)
AND Mean_&_Median (Terraced, 35, 37)
AND 1st_&_3rd_Quartiles (Terraced, 22, 49)
AND Percentage_PurposeBuiltFlats is inRange (0, 18)
AND Mean_&_Median (PurposeBuiltFlats, 27, 20)
AND 1st_&_3rd_Quartiles (PurposeBuiltFlats, 4, 40)
AND Percentage_ConvertedFlats is inRange (0, 15)
AND Mean_&_Median (ConvertedFlats, 1, 0)
AND 1st_&_3rd_Quartiles (ConvertedFlats, 0, 1)
THEN Appropriate_Model is HTYPE_4

IF Percentage_HouseholdsWithNoCar is inRange(12, 40)
AND Mean_&_Median (HouseholdsWithNoCar, 30, 31)
AND 1st_&_3rd_Quartiles (HouseholdsWithNoCar, 26, 35)
AND Percentage_ HouseholdsWithOneCar is inRange (46, 49)
AND Mean_&_Median (HouseholdsWithOneCar, 52, 52)
AND 1st_&_3rd_Quartiles (HouseholdsWithOneCar, 49, 55)
AND Percentage_HouseholdsWithTwoCars is inRange(0, 23)
AND Mean_&_Median (HouseholdsWithTwoCars, 15, 15)
AND 1st_&_3rd_Quartiles (HouseholdsWithTwoCars, 12, 17)
AND Percentage_HouseholdsWithThreeOrMoreCars is inRange (0, 11)
AND Mean_&_Median (HouseholdsWithThreeOrMoreCars, 3, 2)
AND 1st_&_3rd_Quartiles (HouseholdsWithThreeOrMoreCars, 2, 4)
THEN Appropriate_Model is CARS_4

explanation with an expert system type of knowledge base.

The conventional approach to building an expert system requires a 'human expert to formulate the rules by which the data can be analysed' (Zurada, 1992: 225). In contrast, a connectionist expert system formulates its knowledge base by modelling implicit functions within a data set. A connectionist expert system is in essence a straightforward neural network. However, the environment software examines the weights recorded for a trained network and attempts to give a tentative explanation of the model based on the magnitude of the weights. Unfortunately, the explanations generated by a connectionist expert system are far removed from the heuristics and processes taken by a human expert. Rule induction systems are another example of methods that have been applied to automate the knowledge acquisition process. These systems learn rules from 'raw domain data' (Quinlan, 1986; Michalski and Chilansky, 1980).

Given the problems associated with direct rule extraction from a neural network structure, the investigation focused on identifying rules that describe the decisions made by the Kohonen network and the genetic algorithm, as opposed to the predictions made by the MLP network. By examining the way the modular system works, it is evident that each sub-model (which in essence represents a homogeneous data set) is constructed using a sub-set of the features present in the parent data set. Moreover, this sub-set of features differs from one sub-model to the next. Therefore, rules extracted by inspection of the feature sub-set describe which sub-model can best predict the value of a previously unseen property. Table A4 shows example rules extracted from the Kohonen analysis of the 1991 Census data, and Table A5 gives example rules extracted from the genetic algorithm model.

The rules describe the profile of an area in terms of selected geo-demographic characteristics. Quartiles are used to give an indication of the core of the profile ignoring tail ends. Although perhaps naive, these rules have obvious links with heuristics used as part of the appraisal process. The rulebase is in effect providing the reasoning for the network decision.

When the underlying clusters for the Kohonen approach and chromosomes for the genetic algorithm approach were decoded in the form of antecedents, the results show that the sub-models contain reference to employment, overcrowding, tenure and car availability. Whether these and similar findings can be reconciled with the heuristics used by valuation professionals remains to be discovered.

A3 Dealing with arbitrariness

Panayiotou (1999) undertook the development of prototype mass appraisal systems of residential properties for taxation purposes in Cyprus. Mindful of the criticisms of arbitrariness in the use of ANNs, he prepared substantial data sets of houses and apartments

Table A5 Interpretation of sub-models in the form of a simple rule-base

Seek Appropriate_Model

IF Percentage_Pop_Unemployed is 'low' (0–2%)
AND Ratio_of_Rooms_per_Person is 'high' (2–4 rpp)
AND Percentage_of_Mortgaged_Properties is 'low' (0–6%)
AND Percentage_of_Local_Authority_Rented_Properties is 'low' (0–9%)
AND Percentage_of_Semi_Detached_Properties is 'low' (0–7%)
THEN Appropriate_Model is 'Sub_Model_1'

IF Ratio_of_Rooms_per_Person is 'high' (2–4%)
AND Percentage_of_Mortgaged_Properties is 'mid' (5–12%)
AND Percentage_of_Semi_Detached_Properties is 'low' (0–7%)
AND Percentage_of_Terraced_Properties is 'mid' (6–13%)
THEN Appropriate_Model is 'Sub_Model_2'

IF Ratio_of_Cars_per_Person is 'mid' (0.3–0.6 cpp)
AND Ratio_of_Rooms_per_Person is 'high' (2–4 rpp)
AND Percentage_of_Mortgaged_Properties is 'low' (0–6%)
AND Percentage_of_Local_Authority_Rented_Properties is 'low' (0–9%)
THEN Appropriate_Model is 'Sub_Model_3'

IF Ratio_of_Cars_per_Person is 'mid' (0.3–0.6 cpp)
AND Percentage_of_Mortgaged_Properties is 'low' (0–6%)
AND Percentage_of_Local_Authority_Rented_Properties is 'low' (0–9%)
THEN Appropriate_Model is 'Sub_Model_4'

IF Ratio_of_Cars_per_Person is 'mid' (0.3–0.6%)
AND Percentage_of_Local_Authority_Rented_Properties is 'low' (0–9%)
AND Percentage_of_Terraced_Properties is 'low' (0–6%)
THEN Appropriate_Model is 'Sub_Model_5'

IF Percentage_Pop_Unemployed is 'low' (0–2%)
AND Ratio_of_Rooms_per_Person is 'high' (2–4 rpp)
AND Percentage_of_Local_Authority_Rented_Properties is 'low' (0–9%)
AND Percentage_of_Semi_Detached_Properties is 'mid' (6–13%)
THEN Appropriate_Model is 'Sub_Model_6'

in the Strovolos Municipality and set about to compare the merits of MRA and ANNs with a MANN, a modular artificial neural network system.

MANNs were defined by Haykin (1994: 475) as follows:

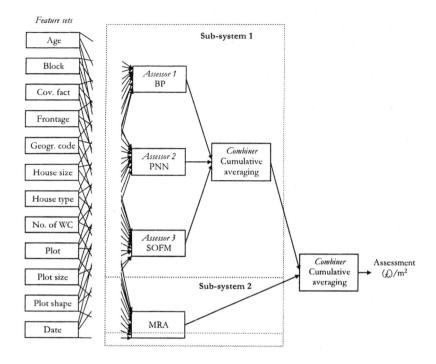

Figure A7 MANN system for houses. Features of the property are fed to the assessors. The results from the two sub-systems are averaged to provide the assessment. (Reproduced with permission by Dr Panayiotou)

A neural network is said to be modular if the computation performed by the network can be decomposed into two or more modules (sub-systems) that operate on distinct inputs without communicating with each other. The outputs of the modules are mediated by an integrating unit that is not permitted to feed information back to the modules. In particular, the integrating unit both (1) decides how the outputs of the modules should be combined to form the final output of the system, and (2) decides which modules should learn which training patterns.

In Panayiotou's model the MANN consists of three neural network 'assessors' (a back propagation network (BP), a probabilistic neural network (PNN) and a self-organising feature map (SOFM) that are combined as Sub-system 1. MRA results are generated from independent Sub-system 2 and combined with the outputs from the neural networks as illustrated in Figure A7.

The best individual assessor was the BP network with 11.41% MAPE (mean absolute percent error) and 11.38% COD (coefficient of dispersion). Second was the SOMF assessor with 12.40% MAPE and 12.06% COD. The PNN assessor was third with both measures at 12.82%. Subsystem 1 produced better results than the individual assessors with 10.77% MAPE and 10.65% COD. MRA produced similar results to those of the BPs. These were 11.40% MAPE and 11.33% COD. The MANN system produced the best results with 10.67% MAPE and 10.57% COD.

The MANN system consistently outperformed individual assessors, Subsystem 1 and MRA.

The case for MANN is compelling. Panayiotou concluded that MANN systems are promising tools in property valuation offering robustness and incrementality, and performance that satisfies IAAO standards.

Note

1. See Lewis *et al* (1997) for a complete description of the process.

References

Clancy, W.J. (1983) 'The epistemology of a rule-based expert system: a framework for explanation', *Artificial Intelligence*, 20, 215–51.

Davis, R., Buchanan, B. and Shortcliffe, E. (1977) 'Production rules as a representation for a knowledge-based consultation program', *Artificial Intelligence*, 8(1), 15–45.

Diederich, J. (1989) *Explanation and Artificial Neural Networks*. German National Research Centre for Computer Science (GMD), W. Germany.

Goldberg, D.E. (1989) *Genetic Algorithms in Search Optimisation and Machine Learning*. Reading, MA and Wokingham: Addison-Wesley.

Haykin, S. (1994) *Neural Networks: A Comprehensive Foundation*. New York and Oxford: Macmillan College Publishing.

James, H. (1994) *An 'Automatic Pilot' for Surveyors*, Cutting Edge Conference. London: RICS.

Lewis, O.M., Ware, J.A. and Jenkins, D.H. (1997) *A Neural Network Technique for Detecting and Modelling Residential Property Submarkets*. International Conference on Neural Networks and Genetic Algorithms, Norwich, UK.

Michalski, R. and Chilansky, R.L. (1980) 'Learning by being told and learning from examples', *Journal of Policy Analysis and Information Systems*, 4.

Panayiotou, P.A. (1999) 'Immovable property taxation and the development of an ANN valuation system of residential properties for tax purposes in Cyprus.' Unpublished PhD thesis, University of Glamorgan.

Quinlan, J.R. (1986) 'Induction of decision trees', *Machine Learning*, 1, 81–106.

Stefánsson, A., Koncar, N. and Jones, A.T. (1997) 'A note on the Gamma test', *Journal of Neural Computing and Applications*, 5(3), 131–3.

Tay, D.P.H. and Ho, D.K.H. (1992) 'Intelligent mass appraisal', *Journal of Property Tax Assessment and Administration*, 10, 5–25.

Zurada, J.M. (1992) *Introduction to Artificial Neural Systems*. St Paul, MN: West Publishing.